BAD MEN AND BAD TOWNS

BAD MEN AND BAD TOWNS

by

WAYNE C. LEE

DRAWINGS BY E. L. REEDSTROM

THE CAXTON PRINTERS, LTD.
Caldwell, Idaho
1993

Library of Congress Cataloging-in-Publication Data

Lee, Wayne C.
    Bad Men and Bad Towns / By Wayne C. Lee.
    p.   cm.
    ISBN 0-87004-349-8
    1. Frontier and pioneer life—Nebraska.   2. Nebraska—History.   I. Title.
F666.L43   1992   92-17951
    978.2—dc20   CIP

Lithographed and bound in the United States of America by
The CAXTON PRINTERS, Ltd.
Caldwell, ID 83605
155017

Dedicated to My Grandchildren:

Robert, Rebecca, Amy, Sarah, David, and Michael,
in the hope that they will learn
to love history.
Right usually prevails against all odds.
Those who have no pride in their past
have little hope for their future.

Contents

III. GROWING PAINS

IV. COMING OF AGE

Illustrations

Preface

In my research of the wild happenings in Nebraska, I discovered that the small towns often produced incidents as bizarre as any of their city cousins.

In the predecessor to this book, "Wild Towns of Nebraska," ten towns were selected and some of the best stories of each town made up each chapter. In this book, I ignored those towns and looked elsewhere. Many tiny towns produced only one good story and some of those are included.

Since most towns could not produce a full chapter of stories by themselves, I broke this book into segments that had nothing to do with any particular region of Nebraska.

The first segment concerns early Nebraska and the trouble that arose between the newcomers and the Nebraska natives, the Indians, who were trying to hang on to their hunting grounds. That time span covered approximately fifty-five years from 1823 to 1878.

The other three segments are divided by time: territorial days, 1854 to 1867; the growing up days of early statehood, 1867 to 1900; and finally the first quarter of the new century, 1900 to 1925.

Many small towns got their stories in this book. They had their murders and lynchings the same as their larger contemporaries, often with as much or even more startling originality and savagery. But it was all part of growing up into a state that today is a vital part of the bread basket of the nation.

Acknowledgments

In the three years it took to gather the stories and the pictures for this book, I received a helping hand from many people. Without this help, the book could never have been completed. My deepest gratitude to the following:

At the Nebraska State Historical Society Research Library, Lincoln:

Cindy Drake, who showed me a treasure of material on the Territorial Days of Nebraska;

Marti Miller, who guided me to many pictures that I needed;

Randy Flagel, who located microfilm for me;

Ann Billesbach also helped me locate material I needed.

Catherine Renschler, Director, Adams County Historical Society, Hastings, who produced stories and pictures of the Hastings area that were exactly what I needed.

Thomas Anderson, Research Associate, Stuhr Museum, Grand Island, who helped me locate both stories and pictures.

Elinor Brown, Librarian, Imperial Public Library, who always found the books I needed and made available to me all the research material in the library.

Russ Czaplewski, Historian and Author, Dawson County Historical Museum, Lexington, NE.

Ila Christensen, York County Historical Society Museum, York.

Lorena Smith, Phelps County Historical Museum, Holdrege.

Lillis Grasmick, Curator, Platte Valley Museum, Gering.

Debra Dophide, Curator, Knight Museum, Alliance.

Jessica Midgett, Assistant Curator, Knight Museum, Alliance.

Alma Edelman, Curator, Hyannis Museum.

Pioneer Trails Museum, Bridgeport.

Gage County Museum, Beatrice.

Hamilton County Museum, Aurora.

Nellie Snyder Yost, Author and Historian, North Platte, who gave me an excellent story with documented details.

Jeffery P. O'Donnell, Author and Historian, Hastings, who directed me to some very good stories.

Gayle Ginapp, Manager, Waldenbooks, North Platte, whose suggestion led to the title of this book.

Gerald E. Sherard, Author of *Historical Sketches of Giltner, Nebraska*, Lakewood, Colorado.

Raymond S. Cannon, Historian, Minden.

Anoma Hoffmeister, Curator, Chase County Historical Museum, who helped with ideas and pictures.

George LeRoy, North Platte Historian, who gave me the results of his research on Keyapaha County.

Ken Wolf, Historian and Deputy Sheriff, Frontier County, Curtis.

Ruby Kahler, Historian and County Superintendent, Frontier County, Maywood.

Last but definitely not least are two who helped me tremendously with my pictures:

Art Duckworth, an excellent photographer, McCook, who made perfect copies of pictures I was able to borrow from people for a few days, giving me the opportunity to have pictures that have seldom been seen.

Jane Graff, Researcher, Seward, and author of a fine series of books on "Nebraska, Our Towns." She loaned me many pictures for my book and saved me many hours of research and miles of driving.

There are others, I'm sure, that I should include but my memory is not good enough to recall all of them. My thanks go to them, as well.

BAD MEN AND BAD TOWNS

I

RED MAN VERSUS WHITE MAN

1823–1878

Red Man Versus White Man

When the first white men crossed the Missouri River to settle in the new territory of Nebraska, they were faced with two potent enemies. One was the weather—hot in the summer and cold in the winter with a good possibility of droughts in both seasons. In the western section of the territory, they didn't even have trees to break the monotony and the wind.

The other enemy was wild and red and the best horseman that the white men had even seen. The Indian welcomed the white man when he first appeared. But he soon saw that the white man was a destructive visitor, and one that would spell doom to the Indian if he was allowed to stay. He would kill the buffalo and plow under the grass that the buffalo needed to survive. And the Indian's survival depended completely on the buffalo roaming free and always being available to replenish the Indian's larder. The Indian became a more feared enemy to the white man than the weather.

Still, it wasn't until a greenhorn lieutenant, barely old enough to vote, crossed words and then bullets with the Indians just to the east of Fort Laramie that the war really started. To the Indians, the lieutenant's actions showed the real character and intention of the white men and, though they killed the lieutenant and his men, they decided that all white men were probably as bad as that young soldier; and the war was on. It lasted more than twenty years.

It was a trying time for the pioneers on the prairies of Nebraska Territory. There were bad men, both red and white, who challenged the pioneers. They survived the test and developed the land into a peaceful, productive state.

Arikara War—Fort Atkinson   1823

When the first white men invaded the red man's world, the red men tried to make friends with their pale faced visitors. The effort faded away as it became apparent the white men considered the land theirs for the taking.

But even two hundred years after the white men began pushing into the Indian's territory, many tribes west of the big rivers still tried to live at peace with their white neighbors.

But there were enough Indians then who no longer welcomed the white men into the Indian hunting grounds that the white men decided they should build a fort along the Missouri River to protect the trappers who went up the river in search of furs.

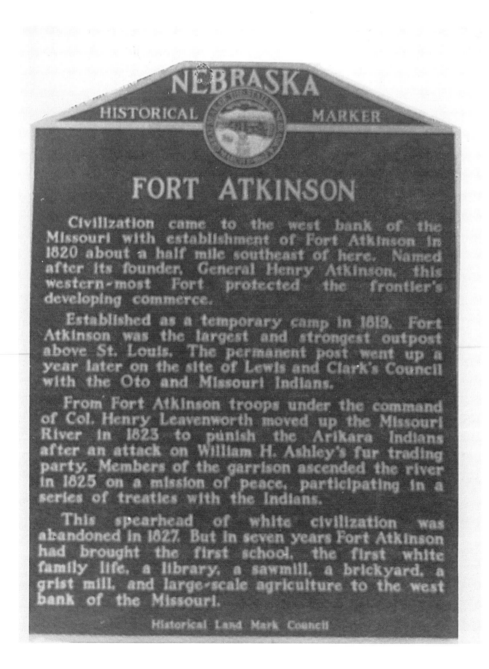

Fort Atkinson marker
*Courtesy Nebraska State
Historical Society*

Fort Atkinson was established in 1819 on the Missouri River about twelve miles north of present Omaha. A small town sprang up nearby which was the first town in the area that would become Nebraska.

The soldiers were at peace with most of the Indians. In fact, they were quite friendly with the Sioux. The first real trouble the soldiers had with Indians came in 1823, and those Indians were quite some distance from the fort.

Word reached the fort that a band of trappers had clashed with the Arikara Indians up the river and twenty of the trappers had been killed. That called for action by the soldiers. Cannons and powder were loaded on keel boats. Soldiers, trappers, and hunters who were at the fort at the time grabbed their rifles and made ready to go out to avenge the deaths of the trappers. About four hundred Sioux Indian warriors also prepared to go. The Sioux were bitter enemies of the Pawnee Indians, and the Arikaras were close relatives of the Pawnees. According to reports, Hiram Scott was among the men going out to avenge his fellow trappers.

The soldiers and trappers marched along the bank. The Sioux followed. Men pulled the keel boats by rope up the river. It was quite a march to reach the Arikara camp. Unlike the nomad Indians, the Arikaras had a village surrounded by dirt walls and fenced with poles set on end. They were farmers and tilled the soil, raising corn and squash.

When the soldiers with their helpers arrived at the village, it was the largest army the Arikaras had ever seen. Nevertheless,

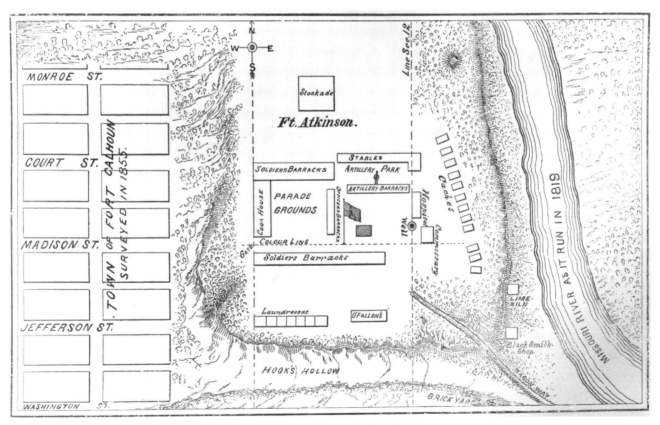

Map of Fort Atkinson, established 1819

Courtesy Nebraska State Historical Society

Little Big Man, Oglala Sioux
Courtesy Nebraska State Historical Society

they put up a fierce battle. The cannons were placed on the hill and fired their balls into the village. The Sioux rushed forward and fought the Arikaras outside the dirt walls of the village. About forty of the Arikaras, including Gray Eyes, their chief, were killed.

When the battle was over, the soldiers, trappers, and the Sioux warriors had a feast of roasting ears from the Arikara corn fields. Then all returned to Fort Atkinson. It was the first battle between soldiers and Indians on the frontier west of the Missouri River. It certainly wasn't to be the last.

Hiram Scott Legend—
Scottsbluff County   1828

No history of early Nebraska would be complete without the story of Hiram Scott. There are as many versions of what happened to him as there are tellers of the tale, and most early recorders of Nebraska history had their own version to tell.

Hiram Scott was a trapper and was returning to the east with his pelts. A consensus of the many versions seem to point to Scott becoming sick. His name was among the one hundred young men General William Ashley recruited for his Rocky Mountain Fur Company. That was in 1822 when Scott was about seventeen years old. His name was on the roster year after year until 1828. In 1827 he and James Bruffee were co-leaders of the caravan to the Bear Lake rendezvous and brought back twenty thousand dollars worth of furs in October. Ashley sent them back that same month to trap more beaver and during the rendezvous of 1828, they took part in a battle with the Blackfeet Indians. There is speculation that Scott might have been wounded in that battle, and it was the result of that wound that incapacitated him on the way back to St. Louis; thus attributing his death to the Blackfeet Indians.

Most versions say that Scott was sick, and two companions stayed with him to help him along. They were to meet the main party at the bluffs on the North Platte River. But Scott was helpless, and he and his companions traveled very slowly. They put Scott in a bull boat, and it overturned in the river; their rifles and powder were lost.

When they reached the meeting place, they found Bruffee and his companions gone, apparently having given up that the three stragglers would ever get there. Scott's companions faced a dilemma. They were out of food and had no way of getting more without guns. If they stayed with Scott, they would all die. Scott could travel no farther. So they rushed off, trying to overtake the larger company. This they evidently did, but they apparently said nothing about aban-

Chimney Rock, best known landmark along the Oregon Trail
Nebraska, Our Towns

Scott's Bluff, where Hiram Scott's body was found

Courtesy Nebraska State Historical Society

doning Scott. They likely said he had died and they had buried him. But many versions of the story say that when they found Scott's bones the next year, identified by the blanket and possessions he had, he was many miles from the place where his companions said they had left him. Perhaps he had crawled that far after being abandoned. No one will ever know.

His bones were found close to the high bluffs that today bear his name. His fate was unfortunate, but his memory will never be forgotten because the bluffs will stand for eons as a monument to the trapper who died at their foot.

Mormon Cow— ## Nebraska Territory   1854

The year that Nebraska became a territory, 1854, the war between the white man and the Sioux Indians began on August 17. A party of Mormon emigrants were moving up the trail on the north side of the North Platte River. There were thousands of Sioux Indians camped along the river waiting for the many good things that the United States had promised them in exchange for a road through their territory.

One Mormon man had a lame cow, and it was falling behind the rest of the train. Something apparently frightened the cow and she bolted off into the Indian camp. The man driving her started after her but decided that he wouldn't be welcome in a camp of that many Indians, so he hurried on to catch up with the wagons and carts ahead of him.

When the Mormons got to Fort Laramie, they complained about losing their cow. The commander of the fort assigned a young lieutenant, barely of legal age, to take some soldiers and go back east and get the cow or bring in the Indian who had stolen her, if that was what had happened.

In the meantime, a young Sioux of the

Sitting Bull, Sioux Chief
Courtesy South Dakota State Historical Society

Minneconjou tribe, had caught the cow and killed it. He and his friends had a feast. To them, the cow was like finding a crippled buffalo. And to a more mature army officer, it would likely have been considered the same.

But to young Lieutenant Grattan, it was stealing. If he couldn't recover the cow, then he'd take in the man who had killed her. Lieutenant Grattan had twenty-nine men and two cannons with him. He was sure of himself since he represented the army. The number of Indians didn't matter.

He went to the Brule camp where he expected to find the cow or the man who had taken her. He found that the cow had already been eaten so he demanded the man who had killed her. He'd take him back to the fort and put him in jail. Jail to the free riding Sioux Indians was a terrible place, and the chief refused to turn over the man who had killed the cow.

The chief at that time was an Indian called The Bear. He confronted the lieutenant and explained what had happened, but he said he could not turn over the young Indian to be put in jail. An older, cooler head than Lieutenant Grattan would have negotiated, but Grattan, confident of his superiority, ordered the cannons pointed at the camp. He told The Bear he'd open fire with the cannons if the killer of the cow was not turned over immediately. The chief swept a hand toward all the Sioux warriors in sight and told the lieutenant he must be crazy. Then he turned and walked back toward his camp.

Lieutenant Grattan ordered his men to fire. The Bear was killed in that first volley, as well as some other Indians. Before the soldiers could reload their rifles, every man was cut down by bullets and arrows from the Sioux.

The Sioux camp exploded. Death of their chief was grounds for an all-out war; a war that was to last for well over twenty years. The squaws quickly took down their tepees and the men ripped into the storehouses where the goods were kept that were to be distributed to the Indians. In a short time, the Indians were gone, leaving behind ruin and the threat of worse to come to the white man.

Pawnee War—
Washington County 1859

Abraham Lincoln was making a name for himself with his debates when the so-called Pawnee War was started with a simple robbery by the Pawnees. A small group stopped at the house of Uriah Thomas, a bachelor living alone in a little hut some

miles from any neighbors. Washington County, although close to Omaha, was not heavily populated at this time.

The Indians were in no rush to complete their business. They took Thomas's money that amounted to $136, which was a kingly amount in 1859. Then they took his land warrant papers, drank up all his whiskey, and finally took his ox team. To make sure they wouldn't be bothered after they left, they locked Uriah in his cabin.

Uriah eventually got out of his little cabin, but the Indians were gone. A few days later, several men came down from West Point and reported that the Pawnees had raided their area, wrecking furniture, burning some of the houses, and driving off all the livestock. Uriah Thomas and others joined the men to hunt down the Pawnees.

They got to West Point without finding any sign of the raiders. But there someone reported that some Indians were just crossing the river less than a mile away. The men quickly planned an ambush to capture the Indians.

The ambush failed, however, and the Indians ran. The settlers fired at them, killing a couple and wounding another. They did capture one Indian, but he tried to escape and was killed.

The news of the killings spread quickly and people flocked to Fontenelle with every weapon they could find. The Indians in the vicinity far outnumbered the settlers and they anticipated a war to run out all the whites.

The armed men organized themselves, then waited for the Indians to appear. The farmers got uneasy. They couldn't afford to neglect their fields much longer, so eventually those in charge decided they would go out and find the Indians and teach them a lesson they wouldn't forget.

There were nearly two hundred armed men, including Governor Black. The cam-

Indian Burials
Courtesy South Dakota State Historical Society

paign was in the hands of Colonel Thayer. There were rumors of ten thousand Indians on the warpath, but that didn't discourage the men. When they finally found the Indians, there were nearly five thousand of them, but they were from different tribes. Some were Omahas, some Pawnees, and some Poncas. The Omahas were outright friendly and the Poncas were not antagonistic. Only the Pawnees were ready to fight.

The Indians wanted to parlay and the whites agreed. They didn't want to cross weapons with that many Indians. Still they stated their terms of peace very clearly. There had been only a few warriors who had caused all the trouble. If they would turn over those braves, there would be no more trouble. If they didn't, there would be a fight. That was brave talk for so few white men against so many Indians. But most of the Indians were against a fight. They turned over the seven warriors who had burned and stolen from the settlers.

The seven prisoners were tied to the back of the supply wagon for the march back to

Fontenelle Store
Courtesy Nebraska State
Historical Society

West Point. They passed several Indian camps, and the women came out to watch the parade go by.

One squaw saw her husband among the prisoners and she grabbed a butcher knife and ran out to the prisoners. She gave her brave the knife and he promptly stabbed himself, falling to the ground. The guards immediately stopped the wagon and rushed to attend to the wounded prisoner. While they were doing that, the squaw grabbed the knife and cut the ropes holding the other prisoners.

The prisoners fled like gazelles. The guards went after them, firing as they ran. The guards came back in a short time, reporting they had killed or wounded all the escapees but they had no bodies to prove their claims.

The men went on to West Point, taking the wounded Indian with them. Part of their agreement was for the Indians to pay for the expense of the expedition that had been launched against them. The money was to come from the allotment the government gave the Indians. But the government gave the allotment money directly to the Indians, and the so-called army campaign had to pay its own expenses.

Joseph Smith Family Massacre— Hall County 1862

There was no trouble with Indians when the German colony, headed by William Stolley, came out onto the unexplored prairies west of Omaha in 1857 to found a town that the speculators who were backing the colony expected to become the capital of the United States in a few years.

In 1854, the Indians had ceded most of the land in Nebraska Territory to the United States, reserving only the amount of land they considered essential for their own living. Now the land was open to white settlement,

but this new settlement was far from supplies, doctors, and everything people had considered essential to their well being.

The speculators were sure that the capital of the nation would move to a spot in the center of the country as soon as the area was populated, and they intended to have a city established for that purpose.

Starting a city a hundred and fifty miles from the nearest supply source was not easy. Starvation and storms tested these pioneers for the first few years, but they had no trouble with the Indians. They laid out their town close to the large island in the middle of the Platte River, and named the town Grand Island for that fifty mile long island. Pawnee Indians stopped by once in a while, and people bought buffalo robes from them. Sioux Indians also stopped by. But the Sioux and Pawnee didn't come together. The two tribes were bitter enemies. In 1860, they staged a fierce battle on the island in the river within sight and sound of the town. But they left the white settlers alone.

There were soldiers up the river at Fort Kearny, but when the War between the States broke out, many of the soldiers were withdrawn from the fort to fight in the east. With the soldiers at the fort a mere token force, the Indians began turning hostile.

The first blow they struck at the Grand Island community was on February 5, 1862. Joseph P. Smith lived on Wood River, about a dozen miles from Grand Island. His son-in-law, named Anderson, lived with Joseph Smith. He had three sons who helped with the work around the farm. The two families had moved from Indiana the year before, and now lived together.

On February 5, they were cutting and hauling logs to build corrals. Trees were fairly scarce, except right along the rivers. Smith had to go over two miles to find the trees he needed. On this day, Anderson's three sons, Alexander, 14; Willie, 11; and

Third Street, Grand Island, 1880s

Charles, 9; went along to help with the work.

They had two teams and wagons. When they had one wagon loaded, Anderson took that load to the farm, leaving his three sons and his father-in-law, Joseph Smith, to cut more trees into logs.

When Anderson returned to the logging site, he was almost paralyzed by what he saw. His father-in-law, Joseph Smith, was dead close to the wagon. There were eleven arrows protruding from his body. Anderson could see that he had tried to protect his grandchildren. On one side he was holding the hand of the youngest, Charles. The boy was dead, his neck broken and his skull crushed. With the other hand, he was holding Willie, the eleven-year-old. Willie was barely alive, his mouth and cheeks split open from ear to ear. He died within minutes after Anderson got there.

He began searching for his oldest son, Alexander, already resigned to finding him dead. He found him where he had apparently tried to escape the warriors. His head was smashed in. The horses were gone.

Anderson loaded all the bodies in his wagon and drove back to the farm. The Smiths had started a little store to supply their neighbors who were too far from Grand Island to go there for every little thing they needed.

Customers were at the store, and in a matter of an hour, neighbors were gathering to go after the Indians who had murdered the four. They went west, and in a dry bed of one of the forks of the Platte, they found eleven Sioux Indians. They were not fighting but were trying to hide.

The vengeful whites captured them. They were only a few miles from Fort Kearny, so the commander there, Captain Johnson, said he'd take charge of the prisoners and he marched them off to the fort guardhouse.

A day or two later, he released the Indians with the remark that he'd rather see twenty farmers killed than one Indian. A dead Indian might cause an uprising, and he didn't have enough soldiers to handle that.

The friends of Joseph Smith were furious, but they learned later that Captain Johnson's decision had averted a miscarriage of justice. The eleven Sioux Indians who had been captured had not committed the murders of Joseph Smith and his three grandsons.

Adam Smith Killed By Indians— Platte County   1863

In the east, the talk was of Gettysburg. In Platte County, Nebraska, it was Indian raids. In the summer of 1863, Pat Murrey had a contract with the government to supply hay for the troops at the Pawnee Agency. Pat hired his brother-in-law, Adam Smith, and more than a dozen men to cut and put up the hay. He took his wife to do the cooking for the crew. They set up their tents and camp on Looking Glass Creek in the best hay meadow close to the Pawnee Agency.

Pat was gone to do some work on his farm near Columbus, leaving Adam Smith in charge, when trouble came to his camp. The day's work had just been finished and the crew was waiting for supper when a dozen Indians filed out of the hills and into camp. They gave the traditional Pawnee friendship sign and the hay crew responded.

The Indians moved toward the cook tent where Mrs. Murrey was preparing supper for the hungry crew. They indicated that they were hungry, so Mrs. Murrey began setting food in front of the Indians. This close to the Pawnee Agency, they gave no thought to possible danger.

But there was one older man in the hay crew who had learned the dialect of several Indian tribes. He listened to the Indians speaking softly to each other and discovered they were Sioux, mortal enemy of the Pawnee and also of the whites.

He managed to get the message to Adam Smith and to Mrs. Murrey that they were feeding Sioux warriors, not Pawnee. They were alerted, but there was nothing they

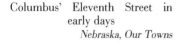
Columbus' Eleventh Street in
early days
Nebraska, Our Towns

could do now. If the old man was right, any move the men made to get their arms, stacked close to the spot where the Indians were seated, would bring an attack. They could only hope that all the warriors wanted was a meal.

The Indians finished their eating and turned with curiosity to the guns stacked beside them. The Indians carried no guns, only bows and arrows. The white men didn't object to their curious examination of the guns.

Then a couple of the Indians began examining a fine team of mules. The old man spoke to them in Sioux, telling them they knew they were Sioux, not Pawnees. The leader admitted he was right, and said they were on their way to steal some Pawnee horses. That was an affront to the men working for the Pawnee Agency, but it was not a matter that white men interfered with; at least, not under the present circumstances.

But when the Indians began untying the lariats holding the fine team of mules, Adam Smith objected. The old man spoke sharply to the Indians in the Sioux tongue. The Indians stopped for a moment then, at a signal from their leader, they dropped everything and whipped up their bows and arrows.

Old Crow, Dakota Sioux
Courtesy Nebraska State Historical Society

One Indian smashed the man who could speak their language with a tomahawk then scalped him. Eight of the Indians shot at Adam Smith, all of their arrows hitting him and dropping him onto the grass.

In a matter of a couple of minutes, the other men in the hay crew were shot full of arrows. Mrs. Murrey grabbed a pitchfork and rushed toward the Indians, trying to stop them from taking the mules and horses. She was shot with five arrows.

The Indians gathered up the horses and mules and drove them away, sure they had killed or mortally wounded all members of the hay crew. They had missed one boy who

had worked with the crew, although not able to do a man's full day of work. At the first sign of hostilities, he had hidden in a big pile of hay.

Mrs. Murrey was seriously wounded but still able to crawl. She crawled to Adam Smith and pulled some of the arrows out of him, but she didn't have the strength to do any more. She crawled a little farther into the tall grass that had not been mowed, and lay there; hoping the Indians would not return.

They were close to help. The Agency was not far away, but nobody there heard any noise. Not a gun had been fired. The boy was too frightened to venture out in the dark to go for help. At dawn, he did run to the agency and reported what had happened.

A wagon was rushed down to the scene. Those still alive were quickly moved to the nearby house of a man named Saunders. There they were doctored as much as could be done. However, all but Mrs. Murrey died of their wounds. She slowly and painfully recovered.

They went in search of the Sioux Indians who had killed the hay crew, but they didn't find them. However, it was a prelude to what the whites could expect in the years immediately ahead, and they had learned not to trust any Indian they didn't know personally.

Bainter's Store—Clay County   1864

While Lee and Grant were fighting battles in the Wilderness, at Spottsylvania and at Cold Harbor as a prelude to the siege of Petersburg, the Indians were striking on the upper Little Blue River as a prelude to what would happen farther downstream on the Little Blue a month later.

Before the serious raids of August, 1864, James Bainter got a sample of what was in store for the early settlers along the Government Road. Bainter came to what would be Clay County on June 8, 1864, and set up a ranch to serve the people moving along the road. It was a prosperous business, and Bainter stocked his ranch with the supplies that travelers would need.

A Pawnee Indian rode up to the ranch in July and told Bainter that Sioux Indians were coming. Bainter had been there long enough to know that there was bitter enmity between the Pawnee and Sioux Indians, and this Indian was greatly alarmed at the approach of the Sioux.

Bainter sent his wife and children east a mile to a place called Pawnee Ranch. To be sure this was a real alarm and not a false one,

Bainter closed his store and saddled his horse, which was a swift runner, and rode to the west. It was several miles to the next ranch in that direction. But when he got close enough to see it, he also saw the Indians. They were destroying the place.

Wheeling his horse, he ran him hard back to his place. There he turned his stock loose, but he knew there was nothing he could do to save his house and trading goods. Then he rode down to Pawnee Ranch to verify the warning that the Pawnee Indian had brought.

Pawnee Ranch was a sod building with a stockade all around it. This could be

Red Cloud as an old man
Courtesy South Dakota State Historical Society

defended. There were several women and children there, and three other men. They prepared to defend the place.

It wasn't long until Bainter saw the smoke up the trail, and he knew that his house, barn, and store were going up in smoke. A short time later the Sioux appeared, 150 to 200 warriors. The battle raged the rest of the day, the women reloading rifles for the men as fast as they fired them.

The Sioux were held off until dark, when the Indians withdrew since they didn't like to fight at night. They were back the next morning to resume the battle. The stockade shielded the defenders so that the Indians couldn't get close enough to rush over them. The sod building wouldn't burn.

Bainter picked out the leader of the Sioux, a chief, judging from his attire and the way he controlled the warriors. As frustration began to get the better of the Indians, they moved closer and raced around the stockade, looking for any opportunity to kill some of the whites.

Bainter kept his eye on the chief. He waited patiently, hoping the chief would come within range. When he did, he fired at him, and his aim was true. The Sioux chief was killed.

For the frustrated warriors, that was the end of it. They withdrew, but not out of sight. However, a short time later, a band of Pawnee warriors came from the southeast. The Sioux, without their leader, turned and disappeared. Bainter had lost his store, but not his life nor his family.

Indians—Thayer County 1864

With the war in the east reaching fever pitch with Grant besieging Petersburg and Sherman destroying Atlanta, it seems fitting that the war on the plains should also reach its apex.

The time was right. It was August, the Dog Days. It was 1864, and all the soldiers that could be spared from the frontier were in the east fighting each other. The place was right. People were still swarming up the Little Blue River and the Platte River on their way to California or Oregon. The road, called the Government Road, was well traveled. Many ranches and farms had appeared along the Government Road because it was considered safe close to that road, and because there was plenty of opportunity to sell anything they could spare to people who, even this close to their starting point, were realizing they hadn't brought some things they really needed.

And the incentive was right. Few people considered the Indian view of the happenings of the last few years. White men were killing their buffalo, plowing up the buffalo pasture, and slicing out farms in the Indian hunting ground. If this kept up, the buffalo would die. The buffalo furnished the Indians with their food, their clothing, and the hides for their lodges. They couldn't imagine life without the buffalo.

So they struck back. The white man's understanding of the Indian way of fighting was that each little group would fight individually. It had always been that way on the plains when white men fought Indians.

But the circumstances now decreed that the Indians had to work in unison. That, in itself, was a total surprise to the whites along the Government Road. Those who escaped the first onslaught could find no help up or down the road. The Indians had struck simultaneously from Denver to the Kansas-Nebraska border, where the Oregon Trail came into Nebraska in Jefferson County. The strike did not extend to much of the Government Road that branched up the North Platte into Wyoming.

The attitude of the white men along this road, and even back from it, changed dramatically under pressure of current

Indian Chiefs ready for the war
path
*Courtesy Kansas State
Historical Society*

circumstances. A quote from the *Hebron Journal*, printed in Hebron, in Thayer County, perhaps presents the settlers' view of the Indian raids better than any individual's description could. This article hit the Journal shortly after the raids of August 7 in 1864:

> From Denver to the Big Sandy, a distance of over six hundred miles, at precisely the same time, along the whole distance, a simultaneous attack was made upon the ranches. No time was given for couriers, no time for concentration, no time for the erection or strengthening of places of defense, but as the eagle swoops down upon his prey, the savage warriors attacked the defenseless white men. No principle of kingly courtesy actuated the breasts of the painted assailants. It mattered little to them that their opponents were in part women and children. All alike were made to feel their cruelty or their lust. No mercy was shown. No captives were taken except women and death was preferred to the captivity that awaited them. Could the Eastern philanthropists who speak so flatteringly of "the noble red man of the west" have witnessed the cruel butchery of unoffending children, the disgrace of women who were first horribly mutilated and then slain, the cowardly assassination of husbands and fathers, they might perhaps (if fools can learn) be impressed with their true character. At morn of August 7, the Government Road was a traveled thoroughfare, strewn with mangled bodies and wrecks, and illuminated with the glare of burning houses. (E.M. Correll, editor, Hebron Journal)

It was a disastrous raid that the Indians launched, with the most lives lost in Jefferson, Thayer, Nuckolls, and Phelps Counties.

Eubanks Massacre—
Oak, Nuckolls County   1864

To fully understand the Indian raids of August, 1864, the situation must be seen from both sides of the picture. The whites were settling along the Little Blue River because it was beautiful prairie country and promised to be a very productive agricultural area. They weren't expecting the Indians to disrupt their efforts to build homes and make a living from the earth.

On the other hand, the Indians saw their prime buffalo hunting ground being overrun by these settlers. The whites were killing the buffalo and depriving the Indians of their ability to survive.

The Indians were not army fighters. They fought in small groups or with their tribe brothers. But the whites could not be driven back by that kind of fighting. The Indians had tried. They knew they had to make an organized campaign against them. Many tribes gathered in mighty powwows to plan their war against the intruders. The raids of August, 1864, and the months that followed were the result.

The hardest hit in these raids was the eastern end of the road they had determined to destroy. Near present day Oak, in eastern Nuckolls County, Nebraska, the settlers and travelers suffered most. Three stations along the road traveled by emigrants heading for California, Oregon, Utah, and Colorado caught the brunt of the initial raids in this area. The trail followed the bank of the Little Blue River and the stations that cared for the travelers were spaced along that trail.

The farthest east of these doomed stations was Kiowa Station, not too far from the Nuckolls-Thayer County line. A few miles upstream was Oak Grove Station, and a few miles farther was Little Blue Station.

The attack of the Sioux and Cheyenne warriors struck all along the trail from southeastern Nebraska to Denver. Their plans had been kept secret. No whites had any inkling of what was about to happen.

The first strike caught a man from Beatrice, Pat Burke, who was hauling a load of corn to Fort Kearny. The Indians hit him close to a place called Buffalo Ranch, just a

Little Blue River near Oak, Nebraska
Photo by author

little to the northwest of Little Blue Station. They shot him with several arrows, scalped him, and left him for dead. He lived until that night, then died.

The hardest hit was the Eubanks family. William Eubanks, Sr. and his son, William, Jr., had brought their families to the Little Blue earlier in 1864 and settled along the creek between Oak Grove Station and Little Blue Station. There is a spot along the creek where the bluffs of the creek crowd down close to the water, called the Narrows. The Eubanks were living close to that.

There were ten members of the Eubanks families near their homes that day. Brothers Joe and Fred Eubanks were putting up hay that afternoon near Oak Grove Station when the Indians appeared. They were both killed before they could put up any struggle. William, Sr. and his young son, James, had just left Eubanks' place when they were caught on the road and both were killed. So William, Sr. and three of his sons lost their lives in the first hours of the raid.

Meanwhile, William Jr. was unaware of what was happening. He and his wife, Lucinda, were entertaining a neighbor girl,

Captives of the Indians—Danny Marble, Laura Roper, Isabelle Eubanks, and Ambrose Asher

Courtesy Nebraska State Historical Society

sixteen year old Laura Roper. William Jr. and his wife had two children, three year old Isabelle and Willie, only six months old.

When it was time for Laura to go home, William and Lucinda decided to walk her home. It was a nice day. They took their two children but left two of William's younger siblings, Dora Eubanks, 16, and Henry, 11, at the place until they got back.

Before they had gone very far, William and Lucinda heard Dora screaming. William wheeled around to see what was wrong with his sister. He ran back right into the Indian raiders. All three, William, Jr., Dora, and Henry were killed.

Lucinda and Laura realized what was happening and they ran to a nearby buffalo wallow and tried to hunker down where they wouldn't be seen. But the raiders, on horseback, saw them and quickly raced over and took them captive. They had no way to defend themselves.

After their fast raid, the Indians left the area. Lucinda and her tiny son, Willie, were taken away with one group as the Indians split up; Laura Roper and Lucinda's daughter, Isabelle, were taken with the other group.

Life as an Indian captive was the worst that a white man could imagine. Laura Roper and Isabelle were released in early September at Fort Lyons in Colorado Territory, after a little over a month of captivity. Little Isabelle had suffered severely in the captivity and was taken to Denver for treatment, but she died the first of November. It might have been her sickness that caused the Indians to release her and Laura as soon as they did. They didn't like sickness in their camps.

Lucinda and her small son were held throughout the winter and were finally released near Fort Laramie on May 18, 1865, over nine months after they were taken prisoner.

One report says that Lucinda told authorities how badly she had been treated by two of the Indians who had come to Fort Laramie, and a colonel who was present had them arrested and hanged immediately.

There were twelve members of the Eubanks family living along the Little Blue. Two, William Sr.'s wife and one daughter, had gone back to Illinois on a visit and thus missed the raid. Of the ten who were there, seven were killed in the raids and three taken captive. One of those, Isabelle, died of her mistreatment. Only Lucinda and her small son survived. It was a terrible price for one family to pay.

Comstock—Oak Grove— Nuckolls County   1864

The Eubanks family members were not the only ones to suffer in the raids near Oak Creek Station. B.S. Comstock had built a fort-like house for his family. The Indians realized that it would take more than a surprise attack to conquer that fort. All along the trail, they had assigned small bands of Indians to attack about noon. But they had assigned forty well-armed warriors to tackle Comstock's fort.

Comstock himself was gone that day, August 7. But there were several men at the place in the grove, including Comstock's son. There were also several women. A visitor from Beatrice, named Kelly, was there that day. He, along with the other men, were

Oak Grove Ranch and Station

Photo by author

about ready for dinner when the Indians arrived.

The red men came in apparent peace and asked for dinner. B.S. Comstock had befriended the Indians at all times, so the request was nothing unusual. The Indians had left their horses about a quarter of a mile from the fort and walked in. That was a sign to the whites that they meant no harm. What the whites didn't notice, or chose to ignore, was the fact that the Indians carried their bows with them and those bows were already strung. To a seasoned frontiersman, a veteran of Indian battles, that would have sounded an alarm. But there were no seasoned veterans at the fort.

The Indians finished their dinner and then were offered a portion of kinnikinnick tobacco to each warrior. On the frontier, that was a mixture of tobacco and willow leaf and bark. If tobacco was hard to get, the bark and leaf mixture was increased in proportion to the tobacco.

Just as it seemed that all were going to settle back and enjoy their smoke, the Indians suddenly exploded into action. They whipped their bows around, fitted arrows to the strings and began shooting. The men were their first targets. Obviously they hoped to take some of the women captive.

The first arrows brought down the man named Kelly from Beatrice. He had a fine revolver in his belt. Two of the Indians dived for that revolver. But Comstock's son was far from immobilized by the surprise attack. He dived for the revolver, too, and succeeded in reaching it first. His first shot killed the lead Indian rushing for the weapon.

The sound of the revolver halted the massacre by the Indians. They had planned on a quick killing then scalping all the white man and capturing or killing the women. A gun in the hands of a white man was not in their plans. They broke for the gate of the fort and raced toward their horses a quarter of a mile away.

Three of the Indians didn't make it to the gate. Young Comstock was very familiar with a revolver and he knew what to do with it.

As soon as the Indians were out of range of the revolver, the whites took stock of their situation. There were still about thirty-five unwounded warriors to deal with. They wouldn't give up. But they fought better on horseback.

Kelly and a man who worked at the Comstock farm, named Butler, were dead. Two brothers, named Ostrander, were wounded. One died later. A boy was wounded but the others escaped harm.

They took the dead and wounded into the house while the Indians were racing for their horses. Then some went to the second story of the house where they had a perfect view of all that the Indians were doing. The others shut and locked the gate into the fort and assigned a man to each corner of the house where they could protect against a surprise attack.

The Indians mounted their ponies and rode toward the fort but rifle fire stopped their charge. Throughout the afternoon, they tried various means of getting close enough

to the house and fort to set them on fire. But the rifles always drove them back.

One Indian on a white pony, braver than the others, tried as darkness fell to get to the wall and set the fire. But he didn't make it. Sometime after dark, a white horse appeared again out in the dim light. One man had sworn he'd kill that Indian if he tried to get close again. He was ready to fire when Comstock's daughter remembered that her father had ridden a white horse that day. She called out to inquire if it was her father returning. He answered that it was. B.S. Comstock came within a second of being another victim of the raid, but not at the hands of the Indians.

Comstock's fort at Oak Grove was the only settlement that survived the raids in Nuckolls County that fateful day. All other defenders either escaped or died trying to protect their homes.

Martin Brothers—Hall County 1864

While the worst of the massacres perpetrated by the Indians in their wild rampage of 1864 was along the Little Blue River in southern Nebraska, they struck at any settlers they found who had ventured out too far west of the Missouri River.

George Martin had established a ranch about ten or eleven miles southwest of Grand Island on the south side of the river. In August of 1864, his two sons, Nathaniel, fifteen, and Robert, twelve, were working some distance from the house. Reports differ on what the boys were doing. Some say they were helping their father load hay; others say they were herding cattle. The latter seems the more likely since they were both riding one horse and apparently no one was near enough to help them when the Indians suddenly appeared on the bluffs to the south.

These were Sioux Indians and they chased the boys. Regardless of what the boys were

Martin Brothers Historic Memorial
Courtesy Stuhr Museum, Grand Island, Nebraska

Mrs. George Martin, mother of Nathaniel and Robert
Courtesy Stuhr Museum, Grand Island, Nebraska

George Martin, father of Nathaniel and Robert
Courtesy Stuhr Museum, Grand Island, Nebraska

doing, they left their work and headed for the house as fast as their horse could go, carrying its double burden.

The Indians shot a lot of arrows at the boys before one arrow struck Nathaniel, who was riding behind, in the back. The arrow hit with such force that it went all the way through Nathaniel and pierced the back of Robert. They were pinned together and they rode on that way for several yards before falling off the horse.

For some reason, the Indians ignored the boys once they were off their horse. They obviously thought that both boys were killed. Perhaps help was coming from the ranch and the Sioux decided other areas offered more safety for them.

Martin Ranch, where Nathaniel and Robert Martin lived

Courtesy Nebraska State Historical Society

Nathaniel and Robert Martin in
later years
*Courtesy Stuhr Museum,
Grand Island, Nebraska*

Nathaniel Martin, holding the arrow that pinned the two brothers together

Courtesy Nebraska State Historical Society

The boys were taken into the house. One report said that the arrow shaft was pulled out the front, going completely through both boys. Few people expected them to live, but the arrow apparently had not struck any vital organ, and both boys survived. Nathaniel, absorbing the full force of the arrow, recovered completely. Robert did not do quite as well, although he lived a fairly normal life, but he died when he was forty-eight. Nathaniel lived until he was almost eighty.

Plum Creek Massacre— Phelps County   1864

The Civil War was nearing its final stages in August of 1864, but the Indian war was heating up. Different reports say that the attack on the wagon train near Plum Creek on the Platte River Road took place early on August 7. Others say it was August 8. Considering the report that the captive taken at Plum Creek soon met Lucinda Eubanks, who was taken captive on August 7 down on the Little Blue near Oak Grove Station, some eighty miles from the site of the Plum Creek massacre, it seems likely that August 8 is right. Indians, even in a hurry as these were after their raid along the Little Blue, could barely have made it to Plum Creek the next day after their raid on the Eubanks family. The time of the raid is not that important; the results of the raid are.

Tom and Nancy Morton lived in Sidney, Iowa. They made a business of hauling freight to Denver. Tom had made three trips that spring and summer, and Nancy had been with him on two of those. In late July, 1864, Tom decided to take another load to Denver. One more load before it got too cold would guarantee a profitable year for his business.

to watch for Indians but to keep thieves out of the wagons. Tom Morton had drawn the last half of the night as his shift, so he was tired. He found a soft spot in the wagon and went to sleep while Nancy drove.

Nancy saw some objects ahead, but she decided after watching for a while that they must be buffalo. They had seen some buffalo along the trail when they had made the last trip. But then as they came closer, she saw that they were Indians. She called to Tom who sat up, startled.

Before they could consider any means of defense, the Indians were close enough to

Freighting outfit
Courtesy South Dakota State Historical Society

In later years, Nancy Morton, who survived the ordeal of the raid and the following captivity, wrote a vivid story of her experiences. They had three loads of freight for Denver. Tom drove one wagon and Nancy's brother, William Fletcher, and her cousin, John Fletcher, drove the other two.

They had few worries about Indian trouble. Everything had been fairly quiet on the plains lately. When they arrived at Plum Creek, eight more wagons joined their three. Any slight worry they might have had about troubles on the road vanished now, with eleven wagons instead of just three.

The next morning, they started out early. They had posted guards the night before, not

swing into two wings to surround the wagons, with ear piercing war cries splitting the air. The teams were halted. There was no way they could get through the Indians.

Nancy realized they were perfect targets sitting up on the wagon. There were bushes down along the streams. She leaped off the wagon to run to them. Stumbling, she fell and another wagon, with the team totally out of control, ran over her. She wasn't hurt as bad as she had first thought. The driving urge to get to the safety of the trees sent her to her feet again.

She began running and bumped into her brother and cousin. They said there was no hope. Her cousin was hit with an arrow as he

Marker outside Plum Creek Massacre Cemetery
Courtesy Dawson County Museum

Plum Creek Massacre marker

Photo by author

said it and fell dead. Then her brother was hit three times by arrows and fell. She tried to help him but a big Indian rushed up and grabbed at her.

She realized then that she had two arrows in her side. They weren't deep and she jerked them out. The Indian demanded that she get on his horse with him and she screamed "No!" He brought his whip around and slashed it at her. The whip lash fell three times before she could get away and tried to run toward the river.

Nancy was only nineteen, but she knew she would rather die than be taken captive by the Indians. She had heard stories of

women who had been captives of the Indians, and she knew that few survived captivity. She would rather die here and now.

Two Indians caught up with her quickly and stopped her. She fought them, but one of them picked her up and threw her on the back of his horse. He led the horse back to the wagons. It was a sight she would never forget. All eleven wagons had been plundered. Some were already on fire. Scattered over the grounds were the dead bodies of the eleven wagon drivers, including Nancy's husband, Tom. Only one other white was alive. That was a boy, Dannie Marble, who had been making the trip with his father. Mr. Marble was dead now.

Nancy cried as they left the scene. The Indian riding with her threatened to whip her if she didn't stop. Dannie, riding with another Indian, cried, too, and that Indian whipped him for crying. Indian children didn't cry. They were taught not to cry when very young. A crying child could be heard for a long distance and Indian strategy usually demanded silent movement.

Plum Creek Massacre Cemetery

Courtesy Dawson County Museum

The second day from the massacre site, one of the chief Indians, wounded in the fight, died. Nancy had to pretend to mourn with the others. She would have been killed if she hadn't.

When the Indians finally reached a camp that they felt was safe from discovery by the whites, Nancy's torture increased. The tribe divided here, and Lucinda Eubanks, who had been captured down near Oak Grove Station, was taken on west while Nancy remained with the other half of the tribe. Nancy was sorry to see her go. They had become friends in sorrow.

They moved again until they reached what they claimed would be a permanent camp. The warriors went out and made another raid. They came back with five scalps and about twenty horses. But the soldiers were

pursuing them this time and they had to move again. Nancy was sure that if the soldiers did catch up with them, she would be killed before the Indians lost the fight. She knew that had happened in other cases. But she would welcome death to the torment she was going through.

The squaws would take the green scalps and throw them in Nancy's face, and laugh when she flinched. When they didn't want to watch her, she was tied up so she couldn't escape.

At one time, they drove a stake deep into the ground then piled wood around the stake along with some dried buffalo hides. They tied her to the stake and began dancing around her, laughing and shouting how they were going to burn her. She shouted back that she'd rather die than live with them. She hoped some Indian would lose his temper and either shoot her with an arrow or split her head with a tomahawk. But none did.

They danced faster and made more threats. Knowing she had nothing to lose, she screamed defiantly. She'd rather die than listen to them. She saw that this was having an effect that she hadn't expected. They wanted her to plead and beg before they killed her. She wasn't cooperating. Finally an old Indian came forward and untied her, saying, "White woman heap brave." They made her step away from the stake then they set fire to the wood and it flared high.

They finished the celebration with a war dance and made Nancy dance with them. Since she had had very little to eat, her strength was about gone. But she knew that if she faltered, they would kill her.

From one raid, the Indians brought a medicine case. It contained several small bottles. Nancy guessed that it had belonged to a doctor. They gave the case to her and demanded that she drink from the bottles. The first one she picked up said "strychnine." She uncapped the bottle. This would be an easy way out. But she saw another possibility. She pretended to drink a little and handed it to an Indian she disliked very much. He took a swig from the bottle and in minutes, he was stretched out dead.

The Indians were suddenly stricken with fear. There were bad spirits in that bottle. They took the entire case and dug a deep hole and buried it far beyond the reach of any digging animal.

The warriors went out on raids every few days, always bringing back some prisoners or some booty. They brought a small girl one time. Nancy thought she was a wonderful child. But she was frightened and cried continually. The Indians could not tolerate that. They finally took her to Nancy and told her to hold her. Nancy did, soothing the little girl until she almost stopped crying. She put her arms around Nancy's neck and held on. While she was doing that, an Indian shot an arrow into her back, killing her instantly.

Nancy was taken out and told to ride a certain horse around camp and not fall off. It was the wildest horse they had captured in their raids and Nancy was thrown off quickly. Her foot struck a rock and broke a bone. But the Indians didn't see that. They rushed on her, kicking her brutally because she had fallen off the horse. Then they discovered her injury and the medicine man took her aside and did what he could to help the foot heal.

After another raid, the warriors returned with the hands and feet of a woman they had killed. They threw those close to Nancy's face and when she flinched, they repeated it. The next day when they moved, Nancy's horse had a scalp tied to the saddle. She knew she dare not remove it but it was torture to ride with the scalp of a white woman dangling against her leg.

They made many raids that fall and Nancy dreaded to see the warriors come back. Sometimes she counted those going out and again when they came back, and she realized they were losing some warriors in the raids.

They returned one day in high triumph. They had a young woman, about twenty, with them. She was a pretty woman and rode proudly on her horse. When they halted, one Indian stepped over to demand that she get down. She drew a revolver that they didn't know she had and shot the warrior dead.

The camp went wild. The woman was dragged off the horse and a stake was driven into the ground. Wood was piled around it and the woman was tied to the stake. Then one Indian slashed the woman on her arms and legs and body. Another poured gun powder into the cuts and another took a torch and lit the gun powder. The woman screamed and wailed in agony until finally an old squaw went over and stood between her

Indians making another raid
*Courtesy Kansas State
Historical Society*

and her tormentors and ordered one Indian to kill her. With a tomahawk, he split her skull and put an end to the torture. Nancy wondered how much more she could take of these Indians.

They were in camp close to Fort Lyon in southern Colorado Territory when she was dressed one day in the finest Indian style and set out in front of her tepee. She had no idea what the Indians were up to until the chief's son came out in all his finery and sat down beside her. He told her he wanted to marry her and the ceremony was to take place right then. She rebelled, telling him she would never marry an Indian.

An array of warriors moved up in front of her, arrows fitted to their bows. A man she called Mr. Bent, obviously one of Charles Bent's boys who lived with the Indians, came over to tell her that she likely would be killed if she didn't marry the chief's son. She told Bent that she would rather die than marry an Indian and she resolutely stuck to her decision. The threat hovered over her for some minutes. Then the old chief came over and called her a brave woman, and said she didn't have to marry his son if she didn't want him.

Bent and his wife, also only part Indian, took her to their tepee and Mrs. Bent told

Nancy that she was sure she would be freed sometime.

Several days later, most of the warriors in camp went out on a gigantic raid. While they were gone, some white men from Fort Lyon came to try to trade for captives. Nancy had high hopes, but the Indians told the traders to come back the next day and talk.

The next day before the traders returned, Nancy and Lucinda Eubanks, who was back in the same camp with Nancy now, were taken into a tepee and staked down to the ground, flat on their backs. Then buffalo robes were tossed over them. They were warned that the slightest noise or movement from either of them would result in instant death. Several men stood close by with bows strung and ready.

The traders came and bargained for an hour for the captives. Dannie Marble, the other captive from Nancy's wagon train, was one that was traded for. Also Laura Roper, Lucinda Eubanks' friend and little Isabelle Eubanks, Lucinda's sickly daughter who died later in Denver, were included in the bargaining.

The traders were satisfied they had secured the release of all the captives the Indians had. They didn't see Nancy or Lucinda, even though they were close to them. The piles of buffalo robes meant nothing to them.

As soon as the traders had left, the two women were uncovered and released and allowed to watch the traders disappearing toward Fort Lyon. Then both women were whipped again, something that Nancy had decided was a daily chore for them. They seemed to get great pleasure from it.

Before the day was over the warriors came back again with more scalps. They had a hilarious time throwing the scalps into the faces of the two captives.

Later that evening a man Nancy knew only as Mr. Smith, a white man who had married an Indian and chose to live with her family, came over to tell Nancy that she would be allowed to go home in six days if the soldiers didn't molest the Indians during that time.

But the next day a scout rode swiftly into camp to announce that soldiers were coming. They had found the trail they had made returning from their last battle. So the camp moved quickly and Nancy did not get her release.

The warriors went out again and they came back with six scalps and about sixty head of horses, but they were not happy. They had run into the militia and twenty warriors had been killed. The chief in his anger told Nancy he would never let her go; they would hold her to get revenge.

Her torture eased somewhat and the Indians kept moving to make sure the soldiers didn't locate them. After Colonel Chivington struck Black Kettle's camp on Sand Creek in late November, Nancy's group of Indians moved north where the soldiers wouldn't be expecting them. They hid themselves in the Big Horn Mountains of Wyoming Territory.

There a trader, Jules Coffey, located them and served as a mediator between the Indians and Major Wood, commanding Fort Laramie on the plains to the south. The Indians were ready to trade for what they needed, and offered to let Nancy go for supplies.

They apparently considered Nancy a prize, perhaps the wife of some important man, because their demand was high. The deal was finally made for six horses, forty pounds of coffee, three sacks of flour, seventy-five pounds of rice, some soda, table salt, a saddle, powder, lead, and twenty boxes of caps.

The deal was almost made when the Indians upped their demands. In addition to what they had already asked for, they wanted thread, combs, butcher knives, tobacco, beads, paints, needles, a rifle, and some revolvers, blankets, and coats. The army finally agreed, and the pile of supplies were taken to the Indian camp. The soldiers got Nancy from the camp in late December.

It was a bitter cold trip from the Big Horns down to Fort Laramie. They made the trip as quickly as they could. They were aware of the Indian trick of recapturing a released prisoner and then going through the whole process of trading again for her release.

At Fort Laramie, Nancy recuperated from her ordeal before starting back to the east. It was February before she began her trip back home, and she arrived in Sidney, Iowa, on March 9, 1865.

It had been a long five months of captivity, each day threatened with death. Nor was the misery entirely over. She still had to adjust to the loss of her husband, brother, and cousin, killed in the initial assault of the Indian raid.

Indian Raids—
Little Blue, Thayer County   1867

After the raids of 1864, the frontier along the Government Road settled down somewhat. Soldiers were stationed at forts and often some were at camps close to the road.

By 1867, it appeared the Indian war was over; there had been fewer Indian raids and confidence had returned to the Government Road. An occasional isolated raid might be expected, but nothing like 1864.

In that respect, the settlers along the Government Road were right. There wasn't another series of simultaneous raids up and down the road. But there was a raid of some significance launched against the white settlements along the lower end of the Little Blue River in Nebraska. This raid was conducted by one war party that swept down the Little Blue.

The raiders began on June 9, 1867, by attacking the Hackney Ranch. Two men, Thompson and Halliday, were at the ranch at the time. They hid and when the Indians could find no one there, they took all the horses they could find, seven head. However, they missed one horse that was behind a knoll. As soon as the Indians were gone, the two men caught this horse and, riding double, got away, hoping to warn others of the raiders.

Next the Indians struck at the Kiowa Ranch. James Douglass was the owner here and he had sixteen good horses. The Indians took them all. Douglass was frantic over the loss but glad that they hadn't found him.

Their next stop was down the valley at the Haney farm. This farm was situated only about a mile from present day Hebron. Haney did not have a ranch like many of his neighbors. He was a poor widower, and had brought his three daughters and all his possessions in a wagon and settled on the little plot of land where he built his home.

The Indians came to the yard where Haney met them. They wanted to 'talk' but Haney knew they'd take his horses. He begged them not to take his team because those two horses and wagon were about all he had. The Indians started toward the house with Haney still begging them not to take his

horses. Then one of the Indians turned and shot Haney in the chest. He died almost instantly.

His three daughters who had been watching fearfully from the little house ran out to try to help their father. For the moment, their only thoughts were of him. With their mother dead, he was their only provider.

But when the Indians pushed them back roughly, they suddenly realized their own danger. With terror adding to their strength, they broke away from the Indians and ran. For reasons the girls could not explain later, the Indians did not press their pursuit of the girls and they escaped from the place.

With the Indians behind them, the girls had no idea what to do next. Their father had done everything for them up till now. They wandered down the valley and finally found a home that took them in. As soon as possible then, they went back to the home they had left in the east.

But the Indians were not through. The

Plum Creek Cemetery, 1864

Photo by author

Indians chased white intruders whenever they had a chance to win.
Courtesy Kansas State Historical Society

next day, June 10, they were still in the vicinity. Captain S.J. Alexander, whose place was only a couple of miles from the Hackney Ranch where Thompson and Halliday had eluded the Indians, decided to go to the ranch and get some of the things Thompson had said he'd left there. Alexander was certain the Indians had left the country by now.

He took a wagon and went to the ranch. He got the valuables that Thompson had left. On the way home, he let his vigilance down when he found a guitar among the things and began strumming it as his team moved along.

Suddenly he looked up and saw eight Indians riding slowly toward him. He recognized their ploy of playing good Indian friend until they were close. He turned the team down a valley leading back from the river. The Indians followed. He turned his team down a side valley then up on a ridge into a second valley. The Indians, still following unhurriedly, didn't reach the first valley until Alexander had gone over the ridge.

Feeling sure he had a couple of minutes, he stopped the team and unhitched one

horse. Jerking off the harness, he mounted that horse and kicked him into a run. He was leaving behind his wagon and all its cargo and one horse but that was better than leaving his scalp.

The Indians disappeared then because they knew there would be soldiers after the killers of Haney. But when the furor died down, the Indians returned to the same spot in August of that year. They found a Captain Hannah and three men driving a flock of sheep to Colorado. They overtook them just west of the Hackney ranch where they had stolen the seven horses back in June.

The Indians killed one of the herders, a German, then set about killing the sheep. The other three herders, including Captain Hannah, headed for safety but had to fight off the Indians all the way along Eighteen Mile Ridge until they reached safety at the settlement at Big Sandy.

Turning from Captain Hannah, the Indians next struck at a man who had come recently from Poland. The neighbors called him Poland Pete. The Indians captured his children, a boy eight years old and a girl, fourteen. They traveled swiftly up the river and the boy grew tired. When exhausted, he began to cry. To an Indian, crying was a sign of weakness that couldn't be tolerated. They quickly dispatched the boy with an arrow in the heart. The girl screamed and tried to reach her brother but they dragged her away and hurried on up the river. They apparently realized how the white men would react to their kidnapping children.

They didn't stop until they came to a cave belonging to two men named Abernathy and Bennett. These two had taken over the cave they found on the land they claimed, enlarged the interior some and built a shed-like entrance to the cave that was made of brush and tree limbs. There was a spring in the back of the cave so the men had running water right in their house.

The Indians discovered this place. One warrior stayed back to watch their girl prisoner while the others sneaked up through the trees and brush that were between the river and the cave. Bennett and Abernathy saw them coming and a battle began. The Indians hid well in the brush in front of the cave and when they met such strong opposition, they set fire to the brush and burned the shed-like approach to the cave. Whether the Indians managed to kill the men with their bullets and arrows or whether the two died from the smoke and fire isn't certain. But the two men were dead when found later by neighbors. They were so horribly burned that they simply sealed the cave and their "house" became their tomb.

A couple of months later the girl was traded for some Indian captives at North Platte and another chapter in the saga of the Indian atrocities along the Little Blue was ended.

Barret Murder—Frontier County 1873

Ulysses S. Grant was starting his second term as president. War worries had given way to money worries. This particular day began with a happy wedding in a new county, but it ended in tragedy; the result of a dream.

On June 4, 1873, Andy Barret and Nancy Wheatly were married. It was a happy occasion, and friends and relatives were there to wish the young couple much happiness and a prosperous future.

At about the same time, something else was happening that none of the wedding party, had they known, would have suspected could affect them; but it did. An Indian had a dream. He dreamed that he had to kill the first man he saw if he wanted to go to the happy hunting ground.

The irony of these two totally incompatible events was that the first person the Indian saw after his dream was Andy Barret and he shot him. Andy died from the wound.

It was the first murder on record in Frontier County after it was organized January 5, 1872.

Marion Littlefield—Valley County 1874

Fort Hartsuff was established in September, 1874. If it had been there a year earlier, Marion Littlefield might not have been killed. It was close to the future site of Fort Hartsuff that a skirmish took place between some settlers and a band of Sioux warriors.

The trouble started on January 18, 1874, when the Sioux warriors raided several settlers along the North Loup River. They hit the homes of Richard Climans and Harry Colby hardest. They stole a cow from Colby. The settlers had no intention of putting up with those raids. The Indians were supposed to be peaceful now. So the settlers banded together and set out to find and punish the Indians who had made the raids. Among the several settlers who went on that mission was Marion Littlefield, a young settler, only twenty-one years old.

Elyria's main intersection, store built in 1908

Nebraska, Our Towns

Fort Hartsuff, built in 1874
*Courtesy Nebraska State
Historical Society*

The settlers located the Indians in the very early hours of January 19. They were camped along Pebble Creek and were having a big feast on the cow they had stolen from Colby.

They opened fire on the Indians, and the Indians, apparently not surprised that the settlers would attack them, fired back. For a short time it was a hot battle. In that time, Marion Littlefield was killed.

The settlers pressed the battle and the Indians withdrew, scurrying out of the territory. Since they always took their dead and wounded with them if they could, it was impossible to tell how much damage the settlers had done to the Sioux warriors. At least, they did run them out of the territory and put a stop to the raids along the North Loup.

George Rowley Murder—
Chase County   1878

George Rowley was just a young cowboy in 1874 when he came to what would be

II

TERRITORIAL DAYS

1854–1867

Territorial Days

In 1854 Nebraska became a territory. Only the southeast corner of the new territory caught some of the civil strife that gave its neighbor to the south the name of Bloody Kansas.

The Indian menace for the most part stayed in the central and western parts of the territory. In general, white men didn't venture too far to the west except on the wagon road that followed the Platte River to the west toward California, Oregon, Utah, or Colorado. Soldiers were out there trying to protect the travelers and a few venturesome people who did go beyond the reaches of civilization, but most civilians stayed close to the eastern border.

The people there had their troubles, but not much of it was with Indians. Now most of their problems were among themselves. They jumped claims, they killed for this reason, or for that reason, and sometimes for practically no reason at all. As the population grew, the Civil War came and went, and most of the Indian wars were pushed beyond the territorial borders. The people, looking forward to becoming a state, had a sometimes violent struggle to outgrow the knee-pants stage of a territory.

Claim Jumpers—
Washington County   1855

Only a year after Nebraska Territory was opened to white settlement along the Missouri River, claim jumpers were active. With all that open land, there were still men who would rather claim land someone else had taken than take free land of their own.

John Goss owned a farm in Iowa right on the river. When the land across the river was opened up, he staked out a claim directly across from his farm which included the site of the abandoned Fort Calhoun, but he neglected to file his claim. He erected a cabin on the site of the fort and donated most of his claim to a town site company which promised to build a new town there.

Newcomers poured in and settled on the town site or close by. A surveyor, E.H. Clark, platted the town then made a contract with the town company to build a hotel for a nine percent share in the town. The hotel would be an L shape, each wing being twenty-four feet by forty-eight feet. It was quite a project, and he paid little attention to what was going on around him.

Then one day he was given a notice by Charles D. Davis, who had quietly moved into the claim cabin and filed a claim on the entire town site. Now he demanded that Clark vacate the area, leaving the almost completed hotel where it was. Clark ignored him, but Davis filed a suit against him.

Davis collected a hundred dollars from Clark for trespassing. But the citizens of the new town were outraged. They tried to evict Davis, but he had the legal papers allowing him to stay and claim the town.

The men got together and decided they had to evict Davis forcibly if no other method worked. This town site did not belong to Davis, not matter how legal his claim was.

So they marched on the cabin to forcibly

Schuyler, one time Nebraska cowtown
Nebraska, Our Towns

throw Davis out. John Goss, who had originally staked out the claim, was in the lead and he was the first one shot. He died on the spot. H.S. Purple, one of the members of the town company was shot in the shoulder and a Mr. Thompson was hit in the thigh. The men had to retreat. Since Davis had filed a legal claim, which Goss had not, the law was behind Davis in protecting his claim. But the story did not end there. There were other ways to make life miserable for Davis, the claim jumper, and the people of the new town took advantage of them. By November, Davis was glad to make a token sale and release his claim to the town company.

Shortly after Davis left, Isaiah Peterson jumped the claim of a Mr. Coon, who had settled close to Fort Calhoun. Coon went to talk to Peterson and was found dead a short time later, shot through the heart. Men caught Peterson and arrested him. There was talk of lynching to put an end to this claim jumping. But before anything developed from this talk, Peterson managed to escape and Fort Calhoun heard no more of him.

Mr. Coon was buried where he fell. He was the first man buried in the county. John Goss, who had been killed the fall before in trying to evict Charles Davis, had been taken back across the river to his old home and buried there.

Hill Murder—Colfax County 1855

In the spring of each year, the Platte River usually flooded. That often caused two or three weeks delay for wagons coming from the Omaha-Council bluff area, wishing to cross the river to proceed on their way west. The Platte River forms the southern boundary of Colfax County and a popular crossing was established there.

In the spring of 1855, a thousand wagons piled up on the north bank of the Platte waiting to cross over. As each wagon came in, the owner was given a number so he knew his place in the line. It was meant to prevent trouble because there were always those people who felt they had a right to be first to cross, even if they were near to the last to get there.

The plan worked quite well. The people observed the rights of those who had waited longest to be the first to cross the river as soon as the water receded enough that it was safe to cross.

There was a ferry here at this crossing. It took some of the animals across and, quite often, carried the women. The men drove their wagons and hoped the strong current didn't roll the wagons over.

A man named Hill was the last one to cross the river the first day that it was deemed safe. The last boat load to cross on the ferry carried Hill's cows. One of the calves panicked as the boat started across and it jumped over the edge and waded back to the north shore. As soon as the cows were unloaded on the south shore, the calf's mother plunged into the river and swam back to the north side.

Hill crossed back, too, to look for his cow and calf. He found them without much trouble. He knew the cow would swim over if she saw her calf being taken over. So he went to the first wagon that would cross the river the next morning to ask the driver if he would put the calf in his wagon.

Hill had needed extra courage to make the crossing himself this afternoon so he had turned to the bottle to get that courage. He was still well "lubricated" when he found his cow and calf and began looking for a way to get his calf across the river the next morning.

Two men, the Brady brothers, owned the first two wagons that would cross the river in the morning. It was one of them that Hill approached with his request. That Brady asked him why he hadn't kept his cow over there when he had her there.

Hill, still drunk enough not to be able to think straight, lost his temper and began swearing at the man. Brady didn't take kindly to the names Hill was calling him and he picked up a wagon wrench and hit Hill on the side of the head, knocking him down and breaking his cheek bone.

Hill jerked himself up to a sitting position and clawed a gun out of his pocket. He shot Brady, but, in his condition, his aim was not too accurate and he hit Brady in the arm.

The other Brady brother got into the fight then, lunging forward and knocking Hill down again. He jerked the gun out of Hill's hand and shot him in the head, killing Hill instantly.

The murderer was quickly arrested by those close by. Justice Kemp lived only two miles away, so they took Brady there to hold his trial. The justice had likely never faced a case of this magnitude. Murder was a serious charge.

He listened to the eye witnesses report what they had seen. The justice sat beside his stove and spat on it several times as he considered the evidence that had been presented. Finally, he made his decision.

"Ain't no cause for action."

The case was closed so far as he was concerned and the wagon train moved on.

Whitmore Scare— Cass and Lancaster Counties 1856

Only one man was killed in what was tagged the "Whitmore scare." That killing took place over in the Salt Basin in early summer of 1856, near the place where Nebraska's state capital would be someday. The Indians had raided a settler's home and in the process had killed the man.

Whitmore lived in that vicinity and he loaded up his family and fled to the east toward Plattsmouth. With each turn of the wheels toward the river, the story grew. Whitmore told every settler he saw about the rampaging Indians. By the time Whitmore reached Plattsmouth, it was a "sworn fact" that the Indians were on a wild killing spree. Already dozens of settlers had been killed and the Indians were heading for the river to kill everyone on the west side of the Missouri.

It had been only two years since the white men had first been allowed to settle on the west side of the river and everybody was still skittish. It wasn't hard to make the people of Plattsmouth believe Whitmore's story. In fact, Whitmore himself probably believed it. He hadn't stayed in the Salt River valley long enough to know that the killing had been only an isolated raid.

The people of Plattsmouth send word to Omaha and Nebraska City and all points between that they had a terrible uprising on their hands and a total military effort would be needed to quell it. Weeping Water to the southwest of Plattsmouth was chosen as the

South Fifth Street, Plattsmouth

Courtesy Nebraska State Historical Society

staging point for the campaign against the savage hordes.

Omaha sent men and Nebraska City sent men and almost every able bodied man in Cass County went to Weeping Water until they had amassed about five hundred armed men ready to defend their homes. General Thayer sent a six-pound cannon from Omaha to Plattsmouth on the boat, "St. Mary's." Then he immediately followed it, taking command of the five hundred fighting men ready to go on the campaign.

Scouts were sent out as far as the Salt Basin. They returned at dark with one prisoner, the only Indian they had seen. But now that they had a prisoner, they were sure that the Indians would strike in an effort to get him free.

Pickets were placed around the camp. One man, carrying a musket, was very nervous and tried to see in all directions at once. Every time he wheeled, the air whistled over the musket barrel, causing a whisper that the guard was sure was the flight of an arrow. That arrow had missed him but he just knew the next one would kill him.

About midnight one guard was sure he saw Indians creeping up. The night was chilly with a sharp north wind blowing and the surrounding cottonwoods were adding to the eeriness of the night with their moaning in the wind. The guard's cry of "Indians!" brought every man out of his blankets.

As one man reported later, most of the men were in precariously exposed positions because there were hardly enough trees for the officers to hide behind. Then they discovered that the "Indians" were an acre of tree stumps which they had seen the day before but had somehow mysteriously become prowling Indians in the dim night light.

To top off their night, the Indian prisoner got sick and five guards walked him around until he recovered. But the Indian took advantage of this semi-freedom and dived over the bank of Weeping Water Creek and vanished like a fog in hot sunshine.

When morning came, the disgruntled army, with no sign of any Indians, headed for home. The cannon which had been shipped to Plattsmouth never got out to Weeping Water. Nor did it get back to Omaha to General Thayer who had sent it down to Plattsmouth.

Omaha called for the cannon because they wanted it to touch off the 4th of July celebration. But Plattsmouth said they couldn't find the cannon. They didn't find it until sun-up on the 4th when it bellowed out its six-pound welcome to the big celebration. On July 5, the cannon was sent back to Omaha.

Winter of '57   1856-1857

We seldom attribute murders to storms, but we do have killer storms. One of the worst ever in Nebraska struck in early December, 1856. It began on the first day of December with rain. Then the wind switched to the northwest and the rain became sleet, then snow. The wind rose and the temperature dropped out of sight.

One man writing of the winter, after it was over, called it ninety blocks of ice, one for each day from December 1 to February 28. Just how bad it was out on the plains and prairie to the west was never really known. There were very few people any distance from the Missouri River. But it was terrible along the river. One man lost his cattle when the blizzard hit and didn't find them until late February. Only a few were still alive and they had survived by eating bark and branches of trees. They were still trapped in a small canyon when they were found.

Nebraska City reported that wolves ran deer through the streets of the town, both wolves and deer so thin and weak that the

Hauling corn, an all-winter-long
job
Nebraska, Our Towns

chase was not very swift. Thirty-foot-deep draws were filled level with snow. One settler, lost at the beginning of the storm, was not found until early April. They held his funeral then, over four months after he died.

Records have been kept up to the present and they show that no winter since has had as much snowfall as the "Hard Winter," the winter of 1857.

Myers Killed By Negroes— Nemaha County Fall   1857

Slavery was a very touchy subject in southeastern Nebraska Territory just before the big war that rejected slavery. A man named Archie Handley rode into Brownville one day and reported that he had seen three Negroes pass his house, going north, and they were heavily armed.

The slave owners over in Missouri had posted a standing offer of one hundred dollars for any slave returned to them. Even a free Negro had to stay clear of the hunters who were out to grab that money by returning any Negro they found to the men in Missouri. Unless he could find white men

who would swear he was a free Negro, he could quickly become a slave again.

Handley was one of those hunters, and he had no trouble finding other men who were eager to earn that money. Three hundred dollars was a lot of money to men who seldom earned that much in a year.

Handley carefully picked three men to go with him. Clark, Williams, and Myers were all pro-slavery sympathizers, and this was an opportunity to earn money while helping those whose cause they supported.

Men poured out of town and began searching along the river and farms. Handley and his companions located a thicket close to the river and surmised the Negroes might be hiding there. By now, the Negroes must know that men were searching for them. Cautiously, they worked their way into the thicket.

They found the three fugitives resting in a secluded spot. But they were not surprised by the hunters. They had their guns in their hands. A battle erupted, almost close enough to be a hand-to-hand fight. One Negro was shot through the wrist. But the whites were

Dray wagons lined up at the depot loading dock
Nebraska, Our Towns

bested. Myers was seriously wounded and the four men retreated. Myers soon died.

The Negroes quickly drove the white men away from the horses, took three of the horses and anything the hunters had that they wanted, and rode north. The wounded Negro was soon so sick and weak that the other two had to leave him close to a house and they rode on, making good time on horseback. They escaped but they left a turmoil behind them.

The people in the house where the Negro had been left found him and they took him to town and turned him over to a doctor. They wanted no part of the trouble a runaway slave could cause them. The doctor had to amputate the lower arm of the Negro. Then he turned him over to the deputy sheriff, Ben Thompson, for safe keeping. Thompson took him to a boarding house called the American House and stayed there with him.

News of what had happened flashed across the river and a mob of Missourians came across to take care of the Negroes and the Abolitionists who aided them. They would avenge the death of Myers.

They learned where the deputy sheriff was holding the wounded Negro and went to the American House and demanded the Negro. Thompson refused to give him up. They swore they would hang the Negro and they would drive the Abolitionists out of town.

They didn't press the matter then but they came back after dark and demanded admittance to the American House. Thompson warned them to go away. They shouted that they'd break down the door if he didn't open it. Thompson promised them that there would be several funerals over in Missouri if they tried it.

The Missourians believed him but they didn't leave town. They only waited for more help to come from across the river. The Free Staters realized this could erupt into a small war. They organized themselves and warned the pro-slavery Missourians to go home. Toward evening the next day, they did; and quiet prevailed again in Brownville.

Noonan Murder—Douglas County 1858

Disputes over ownership of claims erupted with frightening frequency in the years after the land on the Nebraska side of the river was opened to settlement. A man named Noonan had come across the river shortly after the opening and took a claim near the confluence of the Elkhorn and Platte Rivers.

Noonan didn't stay on his claim all the time. He also had a home in Cuming City to the east near the Missouri River. Perhaps the fact that Noonan wasn't living every day on his claim encouraged a man named Mathews to decide he could jump that claim.

Noonan found Mathews on his claim and attempted to push him off. Mathews insisted it was his claim. They sent the dispute to the court. The land office at that time was in Cuming City. Both Noonan and Mathews were present at the hearing and they exchanged some hot words. It was apparent that there was no love wasted between the two.

Until the case was settled, Mathews clung to his hold on the claim and Noonan lived in his town house. On Sunday before the court was to hand down its final decision, Noonan decided to go out to his claim. He expected Mathews to be gone; at least, until the court ruled on the case. He was gone that night so Noonan spent the night in his house on the claim.

The next morning he went to visit a neighbor. While he was there, Mathews came by with a rifle over his shoulder. When he saw Noonan, he began shouting at him. Noonan gave back as good as Mathews sent. Mathews, incensed, swung his rifle around and shot Noonan in the chest, killing him almost instantly.

Noonan was about thirty-five years old and left a wife and several children. Mathews was considered a peaceful inoffensive man by those who knew him. But now he faced a court decision far more important to him than the settlement of the ownership of a claim.

Levitt Lynching—
Richardson County   1858

Nebraska Territory had a Criminal Law by which it was governed but in 1858, the Criminal Law was repealed. The result was that anyone could do about as he pleased without fear of any legal punishment or reprisal. In a land where horses were both a mark of wealth and essential to survival, this led to many sudden unauthorized changes of ownership among horse lovers.

With no legal means to stop horse stealing, the men who cherished their own horses and not those of their neighbors banded together and formed a committee to watch for those who didn't adhere to those principles. There were about two hundred men in the Vigilance Committee in Richardson County. The leader was Sheriff Wilson Maddox. His legal authority was sharply curtailed by the repeal of the Criminal Law but, with two hundred men behind him, he carried an authority he had never had before.

Their method of discouraging such flagrant disregard of ownership was to tie the thief, once he was caught, then bind him to a sturdy tree and let each member of the committee give the man a half dozen lashes with a hickory withe if he wished. Those who had lost horses to the thieves were eager to take their turn. Often when the whipping was over, they could see deep cuts in the bark of the tree where the whip had curled around the tree after striking the culprit. One trip through that punishment was usually enough to cure any covetous horse thief.

But occasionally there was one who went back to his trade. The second time he was caught, he not only got the lashings from the hickory withe but he also got a generous coat of hot tar and feathers.

Even that was not enough to convince one stubborn thief named Levitt. When it was proven that he was still stealing horses after

Wahl Block in Falls City, Richardson County

being reprimanded twice by the gentle hands of the Vigilance Committee, they sent their leader, Sheriff Maddox, out to bring him to final justice.

Levitt lived southwest of Falls City. Maddox took several committee members with him when he went after Levitt. Levitt decided Nebraska was not a comfortable place for him to be just then so he crossed the river into Missouri. Maddox forgot that he was a sheriff, limited to the confines of his county. He was after a horse thief and a river or a state line wasn't going to stop him. They caught up with one of Levitt's men at a farm house and soon located Levitt himself in a corn field.

Maddox stationed his men all around the cornfield and then he went into the field himself to flush out the thief. Everything was going well until one of the men at the edge of the field accidentally fired his gun. The shot served as a signal to the others that the thief had been located where the gun had been fired and they rushed to the spot. That left areas of the field perimeter unguarded and Levitt escaped.

Maddox got the promise of the Missouri authorities to watch for Levitt then took his men back across the river. The Missouri authorities did find Levitt and arrested him but he escaped again. But then authorities in Missouri and Iowa caught him again and this time they delivered him to St. Stephens over on the Nebraska side of the river.

Sheriff Maddox called for a jury of men and they tried Levitt. It was a short trial.

Everybody knew what Levitt had been doing. Levitt himself did not deny it. But he was surprised at the verdict of the jury. Under the circumstances, the jury said, since all punishment had been ignored, he should be hanged.

At first Levitt treated the verdict as a bad joke. He expected another whipping and perhaps another coat of tar. But the joke faded when they tied his hands and feet instead of tying him to a tree. They placed him in a wagon and drove a half mile out of town to a hollow where a big tree stood. Levitt was made to stand on a box in the wagon and the noose slipped over his head. Then the wagon was driven out from under him.

Levitt's lynching had a strong effect on horse stealing in Richardson County. As one man expressed it, "Horse stealing became unpopular."

Lynching—Douglas County   1859

In the winter of 1858–59, two men, John Daley and Harvey Braden, were doing a lot of horse trading with horses that weren't their own. They were caught and taken to the jail in Omaha. Since this was an occupation definitely frowned upon by the good citizens of Omaha and especially by the horse owners whose horses were the objects of the transactions, it was decided that something had to be done. Legal procedure was too slow and often netted unsatisfactory results.

Sheriff Reeves, who lived in rooms above the jail, was out of town and had given the keys to the jail to three women who were watching the jail until his return. Those who had decided that justice could best be served by administering it themselves moved up to the jail on the night of January 10, 1859, forcibly took the keys from the three ladies, and unlocked the jail.

Over the objections of the two prisoners, they dragged the horse thieves out of the jail and put them into a wagon. Then they drove north two miles beyond Florence and there, using a convenient tree, they demonstrated what they considered true justice.

First Nebraska Capitol, Ninth
Street, Omaha
Nebraska, Our Towns

As a reminder to any other would-be horse thieves what they could expect, they brought the bodies back into town the next afternoon, Sunday, January 9, and laid them out on the ground in front of the courthouse door. It was a shock to all who witnessed the scene. Whether any potential horse thieves saw it or not was not uppermost in the minds of the citizens who did.

A jury of men quickly came together, ten in all, and examined all the facts available concerning the deaths of the two prisoners. Knowing four of the men who were in the lynch mob (apparently the ones who brought the bodies back to town), they handed down a verdict of murder against William Conner, Thomas Allen, Rufus Bryant, and Joseph Seeley.

The four men were rounded up. Others in the mob were unknown and the four did not reveal their names. These four were sent to Sarpy County for trial. It was too hard to find a jury of men in Douglas County who had not already made up their minds about the situation.

Daniel Hudgins Murder— Richardson County   1859

Down in Richardson County in the southeast corner of the state, near the little town of Salem, an argument arose over a claim. Arguments over land claims were nothing new in the first ten years of the Territory's existence. The thing that made this argument stand out was the way it was resolved.

Daniel Hudgins and a man whose name has slipped through the cracks of history claimed the same piece of land and they each stood firm on his resolution to hold it. What started as a fairly intelligent disagreement grew into a hot exchange of words.

Hudgins, who apparently had no intention of getting into a physical demonstration of his disagreement with the other man finally let his temper snap and he swung his cane, hitting the other man a rather severe blow on the head.

Realizing what he had done, he turned and beat a hasty retreat from the scene. This would suggest that Hudgins' opponent was a bigger, stronger man and Hudgins wanted no part of a fight with him.

The problem was that Hudgins hadn't hit the man hard enough to take him out of the fight. He got up quickly and took after Hudgins. The pursuit got close and all Hudgins had with which to defend himself with was his cane.

The other man was wielding a big knife and just as Hudgins turned to see how close the man was, he swung the knife with all the force he had. The blade cut Hudgins' throat from ear to ear. He fell dead on the spot and the argument was over.

Higgins Murder   1860

M.W. Higgins was a freighter for Russell and Waddell. He was in a train that was returning to Nebraska City from the mines in Colorado. It was January of 1860 and the mines were new along the front of the mountains in western Kansas Territory. The city of Denver was little more than a hodge-podge of shacks along the banks of Cherry Creek.

They were about a hundred miles from Nebraska City when Higgins discovered a man hiding in his wagon. He had apparently hidden there when they left the mines. Higgins could only guess that he was running from someone or something.

Inquiry brought out the name of the man, Henry Scroggins. Higgins asked him to get out of his wagon; he wasn't carrying passengers. Scroggins refused to budge.

Higgins asked the freighters near him as well as the captain of the train, Captain

Donaldson, what he should do. They agreed that Scroggins should be put out of the wagon. At least, he could walk the rest of the way to Nebraska City.

Higgins climbed back into his wagon and attempted to make Scroggins get out. Scroggins pulled a long knife from beneath him and with a hard thrust, stabbed Higgins in the heart. He died almost instantly.

Then when others started to Higgins' rescue, Scroggins grabbed a double barreled shotgun and stood them off. Captain Donaldson then took command. He assigned his men to surround Scroggins and disarm him. Confronted with several freighters, most of them armed, Scroggins gave up. Captain Donaldson ordered him tied up and they took him on to Nebraska City with them.

At Nebraska City, he was taken before the mayor. His plea was that he was drunk when he killed Higgins but another driver on the train said he was sober and the act was deliberate murder.

However, there was no law on the Territorial books that allowed them to hold the prisoner so he was turned loose, as one driver said, "to murder again with impunity."

Meeks-Davis Double Murder— Richardson County   1860

The county of Richardson, Nebraska Territory, was established in 1855 and the settlement of Archer arbitrarily selected as the county seat. However, it was moved to Salem the next year. But turmoil over the permanent site of the county seat continued. Finally, in the spring of 1860, the territorial government decreed that an election should be held to determine once and for all where the county seat would be.

By this time, Salem and Falls City were the main contenders. Salem had been the county seat for four years but Falls City was growing rapidly and insisted it was the coming metropolis of the county and should have the seat of government. Both were close to the south side of the county but Falls City was nearer the center.

It took three elections to finally settle the issue. On the day of the third election, April 16, 1860, the day started calmly enough as the polls opened. However, neither group trusted the other. Each sent men to watch the polls in the precincts where it was suspected that cheating might occur. Two men came to Falls city who were ardent supporters of Salem. One was Dr. Davis and the other a man called Doc Dunn. Falls City had an equally ardent supporter who stayed at home to push his cause. He was Thomas Meeks.

Meeks and Davis got into a hot argument. Davis, although a strong supporter of Salem, actually lived in Rulo, east of Falls City. Neither Meeks nor Davis were men who yielded to any kind of pressure and their argument soon reached dangerous heights.

Both men pulled revolvers but before either could begin shooting, a man named McEntire intervened. Davis told McEntire that if he would hold Meeks, Davis would not shoot. So McEntire grabbed Meeks. But as soon as McEntire had a solid grip on Meeks, Davis shot twice at him. One shot missed entirely and the other inflicted a flesh wound in the thigh.

McEntire released Meeks and got out of the way. Both Meeks and Davis emptied their revolvers and hit nobody, hardly the stamp of professional gunmen. The men then came to grips and began fighting. But the shots had attracted a crowd and several men pushed in and separated the two irate men.

The polls were located near the southwest corner of the town square, opposite the hotel. It was near the polls that the fight occurred. When the fight was stopped, Davis went to the hotel and up to his room. Meeks went to a store and had his wound examined. It was

First hotel in Salem, Richardson County

Courtesy Nebraska State Historical Society

nothing serious. But Meeks' temper was injured much worse than his thigh.

Meeks stormed across the street and into the hotel. He knew where Davis's room was and he went directly there. Davis was not surprised. He had his door locked against an intrusion by Meeks. Meeks kicked the door open and came face to face with Davis. Both men had their guns in their hands.

Meeks shot Davis in the abdomen. Another shot rang out at about the same time. Most thought then that Davis had shot Meeks. Meeks fell, mortally wounded, but subsequent events seemed to bear out the final decision that Dr. Davis's friend, Doc Dunn from Salem, had fired the shot that felled Meeks. Doc Dunn left town immediately with his horse on the dead run.

Meeks died within minutes but Davis lingered until the next day. For both Meeks and Davis, the election was over and of no consequence to either.

Torrey Shot 1860

Not all crime was punished by the law in the early days of the Nebraska Territory. The law was often far away and sometimes too lenient to please the people.

On September 14, 1860, at Fremont Springs, where about fifty people were camped, a man named Edwards got into a difference of opinion with a certain Mr. Torrey. Edwards shot Torrey in the head. It was a serious wound but not immediately fatal.

Edwards had no chance to escape. The shot had aroused the camp and Edwards was quickly captured and tied up. Nothing was done until morning. The people wanted to wait to see if Torrey survived the night. They needed to know if they were dealing with a charge of murder or attempted murder.

Torrey was still alive the next morning and it appeared he would survive, but nothing was certain. Justice, however, could not wait forever. The people were ready to move on.

Since Torrey was alive and in a bit better condition that the night before, the verdict for Edwards was less harsh. He was tied up, his shirt removed, and he was given one hundred lashes with a bull whip. He was then released. There was little doubt that he would remember this for the rest of his life and perhaps he would control his temper the next time his wishes were crossed.

McCanles Murder—Rock Creek, Jefferson County   1861

Rock Creek Station was an important link in the chain of stations that followed the Little Blue River up to the point where the trail cut off toward Fort Kearny. The first Rock Creek Station was built on the west side of the creek which ran into the Little Blue just a short distance to the southwest. S.C. Glenn and Newton Glenn built that station in 1857. It consisted of a small store, a barn, and living quarters.

Rock Creek was a small stream but it was difficult to cross, being quite narrow but with very steep banks. The stream was ten to fifteen feet below the level of the land that bordered it. But it had to be crossed because the trail followed the Little Blue to the northwest. The Glenns sold hay, grain, and supplies to the travelers.

By 1859, the Glenns had had enough and put the station up for sale. It happened that they found an eager buyer. David McCanles had come from North Carolina, headed for the gold fields to the west. By the time he got to Rock Creek Station, he had become

David Colbert McCanles
Courtesy Nebraska State Historical Society

disillusioned about the great hills of gold supposedly just waiting to be picked up. He had met too many discouraged miners heading "back to the wife's folks." The Rock Creek Station looked like a good substitute for an empty hole in the ground somewhere to the west. So he bought it from the Glenns.

McCanles had been a sheriff for four terms back in his home town in North Carolina. He was a big, heavily muscled man whose brute strength had put the fear into any law breaker he chose to bring in. He had no fear of any man.

He brought his family out from the east and prepared to make a living off his trading post. But there was one drawback. He couldn't get a good well on the west side of the creek. It was a difficult job to bring water up from the steep-banked creek. He crossed the creek and dug a well and found good

New Rock Creek Station on east side of creek

Courtesy Nebraska State Historical Society

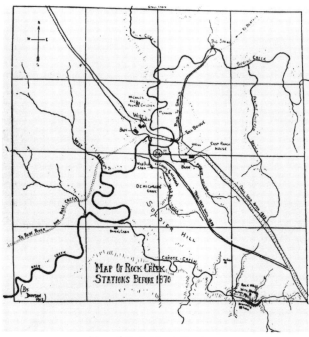

Map of Rock Creek Stations
Courtesy Nebraska State Historical Society

difficulty the travelers had in crossing the little creek, McCanles decided to build a toll bridge. He finished that in 1859 and built a little toll house on the east side of the creek where he collected the toll of ten cents to fifty cents, according to the apparent wealth of the travelers. The travelers were usually glad to pay the toll when they considered the alternative of fording the creek with its almost perpendicular banks.

Things went fairly well with the station and then the Civil War stopped the southern route across the nation and brought most of the traffic north past Rock Creek. McCanles built a lean-to on his store because business demanded a bigger place. Then the Pony Express came through and McCanles had charge of a home station for it.

But the problem then was that the company that owned the stages and the Pony Express, wanted to own all their stations. So McCanles sold out to the company. He built a home for his family on the banks of the Little Blue about three miles south of the station.

Terms for the sale were laid out, so much

water. So he abandoned the west station and built a new one on the east side of the creek. Here he built a cabin, often called the bunkhouse, a stable and corrals, and the station which was part store. Considering the

money down then so much at frequent
intervals until the final payment came due in
mid-1861. The Overland Stage Company
sent Horace Wellman and his wife to run the
station and "Doc" Brink to work as stock
tender.

Early in 1861, the Overland Stage
Company sent a twenty-three-year-old man
to Rock Creek to work as assistant stock
tender. His name was James Hickok. In years
to come he would become known as Wild
Bill. He may have gotten the Bill moniker
from McCanles. McCanles thought he had a
peculiar look because his nose almost
reached his protruding upper lip. He called
him Duck Bill.

It looked to be a most prosperous set-up
for the stage company but the company had
extended itself too fast and too far. Nobody
not connected with the company would have
guessed that the company was almost
bankrupt. When payment on the station was
due, McCanles went to the station and asked
Wellman for the money. He said it hadn't
come through yet.

Then when the final payment was due and
McCanles still hadn't gotten anything beyond
the initial payment, he went again to
Wellman and asked for his money. Wellman
said he was making a trip back east and he'd
get the money. In ten days when he was due
back, McCanles went again for the money,
determined to get it or take back the station.

There is an incident that occurred the
previous spring that is recorded but not well
known. It concerned the father of Horace
Wellman's wife, whose name was Holmes. It
was reported that Holmes stole a team and
wagon from McCanles and some farm
machinery which he loaded in a wagon and
headed south to Kansas to sell it. McCanles
discovered the theft and went after the thief.
He caught him down in Kansas before he
had sold his loot. According to the reports,
McCanles beat up Holmes and brought him

James B. "Wild Bill" Hickok
Courtesy Kansas State Historical Society

and the team and wagon back to the Little
Blue. From McCanles's reputation in North
Carolina where he manhandled any law-
breaker who put up resistance, it was not
hard to believe that he beat up Holmes.
Some claim that the Wellmans were furious
over the incident but were not about to
challenge McCanles. Under the unwritten law
of the time, McCanles could have lynched
Holmes for stealing the horses and wagon
and the law likely would not have dealt
severely with him.

If that incident is true, it would make the
action at the station on July 12, 1861, more
understandable. McCanles and his twelve-
year-old son, Monroe, went to the east station
to collect the money owed to McCanles.
Wellman had just returned from his trip that

Monroe McCanles, David's son
Courtesy Nebraska State Historical Society

day and was supposed to have the money. But McCanles was determined either to get the money or physically throw the Wellmans off the property and take over the station himself. He had never seen the situation that he couldn't handle if he could get his hands on the people who opposed him. McCanles's cousin, James Wood, and a companion, James Gordon, had come to the station with McCanles but they stopped down by the barn.

McCanles knocked on the door and Mrs. Wellman opened it. McCanles asked for Horace Wellman. She admitted that he was there. McCanles demanded that he come out. McCanles had expressed the opinion to his

wife before he left home that he doubted if Wellman would pay off. Maybe the company was broke or maybe Wellman would keep the money for himself.

Mrs. Wellman said that her husband wouldn't come out. This infuriated McCanles. He told her that he'd either come out or he'd go in and drag him out. That was the moment when Hickok showed up. He and McCanles had been on good terms and McCanles mentioned that. Hickok agreed.

McCanles apparently saw something that roused his suspicions. He turned his attention to the movement he had caught. Hickok stepped back into the other part of the room which was partitioned off by a calico curtain. McCanles caught that move, too, and his suspicions grew. He called Hickok to come out from behind the curtain. If he wanted to fight, they'd fight right now.

Apparently Hickok realized that he and Horace Wellman together would be no match for the powerful McCanles. The rifle that McCanles had left there for protection of the station was beside Hickok. He grabbed the rifle and fired through the curtain, hitting McCanles in the heart.

McCanles's son, Monroe, was still there with his father and he said later that his father fell backward out the door on his back, sat up and looked at him as if to say something then dropped back dead. (That rifle was donated years later to the Nebraska State Historical Society.)

Woods and Gordon heard the shot and raced toward the cabin. Hickok stepped out from behind the curtain and into the doorway. He fired twice at each man with his revolver. His first shots wounded James Wood severely and he staggered around the corner of the cabin and fell. Gordon was not wounded so seriously and he turned and ran for the trees along the creek.

Wellman rushed out when the shooting began and grabbed a grubbing hoe. Dashing

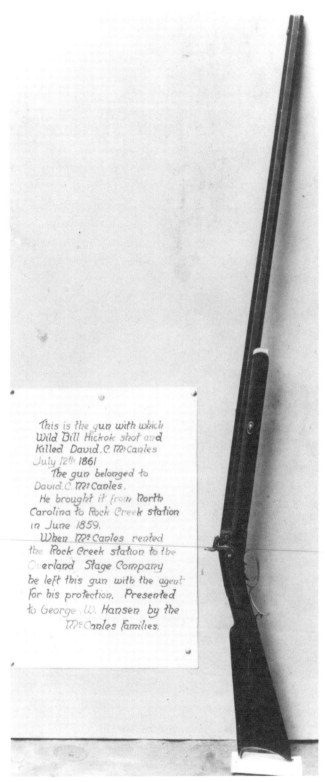

This is the gun with which
Wild Bill Hickok shot and
killed David.C. McCanles
July 12th 1861
    The gun belonged to
David.C. McCanles.
He brought it from North
Carolina to Rock Creek station
in June 1859.
    When McCanles rented
the Rock Creek station to the
Overland Stage Company
he left this gun with the agent
for his protection. Presented
to George.W. Hansen by the
McCanles families.

Rifle that Hickok used to kill McCanles
Courtesy Nebraska State Historical Society

around the corner after Wood, he caught up with him where he had fallen and smashed his skull with a mighty swing of the heavy hoe. Then he turned toward Monroe McCanles, who had been standing as if paralyzed by what he was seeing. Suddenly the boy realized his danger and ran before Wellman could catch him and kill him with the hoe. Monroe headed for his home three miles south where he reported what had happened and said that Mrs. Wellman had been standing in the doorway as he left, screaming, "Kill them all!"

Hickok, Wellman, and the stock tender, Doc Brink, followed Gordon's trail and found him a half mile from the station, hiding in the trees along the creek. Brink had brought along his shotgun. It was used to kill Gordon.

Mrs. McCanles, realizing the odds against her, sent word to David McCanles's brother, James, over in Johnson County. James came quickly, stopping at Beatrice to talk to the sheriff. He swore out warrants for Wellman, Hickok, and Brink.

The three were arrested and taken to Beatrice for trial. The trial was a closed affair, not even Monroe McCanles being allowed in the courtroom. He could have been the prime witness but for some reason, maybe his age, he was barred. The jury brought in a verdict of self defense and all three men were released.

Kansas towns like Abilene might have been different, whether better or worse, if the town hadn't had a marshal named Wild Bill Hickok. And Deadwood, South Dakota, would have missed out on some free publicity if Hickok had not been in No. 10 Saloon that day to be brought down by a shot in the back.

As it was, James B. Hickok, who had never shot a man up to that time, was turned free to become one of the notorious gunmen of the west.

Warrant for the arrest of "Duck Bill" Hickok
Courtesy Nebraska State Historical Society

Ensworth and the Buffalo— Nuckolls County   Summer 1863

Not all the events on the frontier were tragic. In the summer of 1863, while most of the nation was concentrating on the news of the big battle at Gettysburg, E.S. Comstock of Nuckolls County organized a buffalo hunting party. Comstock had two grown daughters and he invited their friend, a daughter of a man named Butterfield, to come along. Butterfield was a merchant from Atchison who was visiting nearby.

They all gathered at Oak Grove and started out for their day of hunting, taking along a picnic dinner. The three girls were special friends.

Miss Butterfield had acquired a suitor in the short time she had been in the area, a dapper young man named Ensworth. It happened on that day that Ensworth decided to pay a visit to Miss Butterfield so he dressed in his very best clothes, which included a fancy pair of doeskin pantaloons.

When he arrived at the place where the Butterfields were staying, he was told they had gone on a picnic. Ensworth decided he would follow and join them for the picnic. He was riding a fine black horse that he admired almost as much as he did his fabulous clothes.

He found the picnickers just spreading out their dinner on the grass about thirty yards from their wagon. Ensworth dismounted and tied his horse to a wagon wheel.

He saw the buffalo bull calf that the party had captured that morning. There were two men in addition to Butterfield and Comstock and they had had a merry time controlling the little bull after they had caught him.

But now the buffalo calf was lying beside the wagon, exhausted from his efforts to free himself. Ensworth, obviously with no inkling of how to treat a buffalo, reached down and rubbed the calf on the head.

The buffalo, totally surprised, reared to his feet. The rage in him at being captured had abated but it had not died. Now he had one of the creatures that had no ignobly fastened him to this wagon right in front of him. He lowered his head and charged.

The buffalo's head ripped between Ensworth's legs and Ensworth found himself riding backward on the neck of the buffalo. The rope that held the calf to the wagon was over sixty feet long and the buffalo, trying to dislodge his rider so he could gore him, charged blindly ahead, shaking his head, which was massive for an animal no older than he was.

He was at full steam, heading directly toward the picnicking party, when he reached the end of the rope. The rope was stout and the buffalo came to a very abrupt halt. Ensworth didn't.

His momentum was such that he shot over the buffalo's head, the stubby horns of the animal catching in the doeskin pantaloon legs and ripping the pants completely off. He landed in a disgraceful heap only a few feet from the girls who were ready to begin eating.

The men roared with laughter but the girls, true to their ladylike upbringing, tried not to laugh. But one couldn't restrain herself and soon all three were laughing hilariously when it became apparent that Ensworth was hurt only in his pride.

The buffalo shook his head until he got the hateful pants off his horns then turned away. The rope wouldn't let him finish what he had started. Ensworth, embarrassed beyond imagination, dashed back around the wagon.

Butterfield found him there. Butterfield was a big man and he had an extra pair of pants. They were twice too big for Ensworth but they did cover him completely from chest to the bottom of his boots. He wrapped them around himself as best he could. The girls were recovering from their laughter and they tried to coax him to stay for the picnic. But he'd had all of the picnic and buffalo hunting he wanted. He rode away, sadder, wiser, and with a totally revised estimate of what a wild buffalo could do.

John Ray Murder—Otoe County   1863

John Ray was a resident of Rockport, Missouri, when he decided to make a trip to the west. The exact reason for his trip was not revealed, or if it was, it was buried under the circumstances that evolved from the trip.

Ray took a young man, little more than a boy, with him on the trip. John Ray's body was found on the trail west of Nebraska City and it was quickly determined that he had not been dead long, apparently having been killed about the nineteenth of August.

Several people had seen John Ray traveling with the young man and they quickly decided that Ray's companion was probably

Unmatched team—a horse and a cow pulling a buggy
Nebraska, Our Towns

the murderer. If he wasn't the one who killed Ray, he surely knew who the killer was.

They caught up with the young man and tried to get him to tell what had happened. He refused. He wouldn't admit he had killed Ray nor would he implicate anyone else. But the men who were questioning him were certain that he knew much more than he was telling.

They decided on a plan to make him talk. They got a rope and led the young man under a tree, put a noose around his neck, threw the end of the rope over a limb and pulled the fellow off the ground.

When they let him down, he still refused to talk. They repeated the process, leaving his feet off the ground a little longer. But again, they got no results. He wouldn't even say he didn't know who killed Ray.

So once more they pulled him off the ground. This time they kept him there until his face turned red and threatened to burst. When they dropped him, gasping, to the ground this time, he realized that the next time they might not let him down at all. He confessed that he had killed John Ray himself. He didn't offer any reasons and nobody asked. They were satisfied to know they had corralled the killer.

Adeline Doren Murder—
Nemaha County 1864

It was the dog days of August and a lecture on Phrenology was scheduled at the town hall in Brownville on August 25, 1864. Most of the town attended. It promised to be quite an interesting evening.

Adeline Doren, a widow who lived just a little over two hundred yards from the town hall, decided she would not go to the lecture. Her daughter was going and she could tell her what she had learned at the lecture. Adeline Doren lived with her daughter.

Sometime during the lecture, a Negro named Warren, who lived in the neighborhood, came over, apparently with robbery on his mind and thinking everybody would be at the lecture. Finding Mrs. Doren at home alone, he demanded her money but she defied him. Grabbing a small ax, he hit Mrs. Doren over the head.

Then he ransacked the house, looking for money, but he didn't find any. He was just ready to give up the search when he saw Mrs. Doren stagger to her feet and go outside. He had thought he had killed her.

Warren chased after the woman, still carrying the ax, and hit her over the head

Many towns had their wells in the middle of the street
Photo by author

several times, making sure he had completed the job. Then he left hurriedly.

When the lecture was over, the daughter came home. She found the lamp still lit and blood on the floor but her mother was gone. It was hard to believe anything serious could have happened when there were neighbors so close by. Of course, most of the neighbors had been at the lecture.

Mrs. Doren's daughter spread the alarm

An early grocery store, 1900
Nebraska, Our Towns

and men rushed out to help her find her mother. It didn't take them long to find Adeline Doren. The coroner was called and he found that her skull was broken in three places and her head was almost severed from her body. He concluded that the work had been done with an ax.

No one could think of any enemy that Adeline Doren had. She was highly respected in the neighborhood. The few neighbors who hadn't gone to the lecture had heard nothing unusual. One did recall seeing the Negro, Warren, going to Mrs. Doren's house but thought nothing of it.

Since it was the only lead they had, they began searching for Warren. They found him after quite a search, hiding in a corner. He was almost petrified with terror. They confronted him with the charge of murder and he quickly broke down and confessed, giving all the gory details of the way he had killed Adeline Doren.

A committee of men was named as a jury and a trial was held there and then. Warren's confession, giving all the details that dovetailed with what the coroner had found, left room for only one verdict. The punishment was really all the jury had to decide. It was 1864, the law moved slowly and sometimes not at all. The jury handed down the sentence to be carried out immediately. Warren was hanged that same night.

Renegade Jayhawkers, Lynching—
Table Rock, Pawnee County
November, 1864

It wasn't easy living along the Kansas-Nebraska border during the Civil War. Jayhawking was a common practice—stealing from the enemy of the Union. Horse thieves picked up on this quickly, Every thief who got caught stealing a horse simply said he was Jayhawking and "made a mistake" in stealing a horse from a Union sympathizer.

This excuse wore thin very quickly as more and more so-called Jayhawkers made "mistakes" and took horses from the Union people of Pawnee County. It reached the point where citizens decided something had to be done. There weren't many good horses left and they belonged to union sympathizers. The Jayhawkers were very selective of the horses they took. So it was Union horses that were disappearing.

The feather that tipped the scales toward action was the theft of one of the finest teams in the county belonging to Andrew Fellers of Table Rock. The neighbors met and tried to decide what they could do. They remembered that Dr. J.N. McCasland had treated a wounded man from Iowa a few weeks before. He reported afterward that it was a bullet wound. There were men in the group who knew there had been a running fight with horse thieves just about that time. So they reasoned that this man must have been a horse thief.

A couple of men knew that this man had gone to stay with Isaac Riley to recover from his wound, and some suspected that Riley might be in league with the renegade Jayhawkers.

The men decided to start with Riley. They went to his place and demanded to know what he knew about the renegade Jayhawkers. When he refused to answer, they warned him that his brother had been killed for refusing to tell what he knew. They had hit a tender spot. Riley broke down and told them where they could find the ring leader of the horse thieves. He lived over in Iowa.

The captain of the Regulators, John C. Peavy, took two men and rode over into Iowa. He returned a day later with two prisoners. One, identified as the leader of the gang, was a Texan named Cotheran. The other man was his co-leader, Isaac Clifton, who lived in Iowa.

The prisoners were locked up in a room in

Waterman's Harness Shop
Nebraska, Our Towns

the hotel in Table Rock owned by C.W. Giddings. Isaac Riley, who had been forced to tell where the horse thieves were hiding, was also grabbed and put in the room with the other two.

People gathered at Table Rock from Pawnee County and from Richardson County to the east. Many had lost horses to these renegade Jayhawkers and now they clamored for immediate justice, more appropriately revenge, for the loss of their animals.

There were saner heads in the crowd who tried to stop a lynching but they were shouted down. Men poured into the hotel over the objections of the owner, Giddings, and broke into the room where the prisoners were being held. They grabbed Riley and Clifton, but Cotheran managed to break away from the men and leap through the window, shattering the glass. But before he could find a hiding place, two shots from the vigilantes brought him down. He was wounded rather seriously, so they brought him back into the hotel and locked him in a room.

The other two, Riley and Clifton, were

marched out of the hotel and down the street to a tall tree with a convenient stout limb. The ropes were quickly prepared while some men held back anyone who objected to the procedure. Then the two were mounted on horses and led under the ropes. The horses were slapped into a run, leaving the two horse thieves swinging.

Dr. McCasland was summoned to look at the wounds of Cotheran, the leader of the horse thieves. He said he doubted if the man would live but he might. The next day when it seemed that tempers would have subsided, the mob gathered again. Their job was not done. Over strong objections of Giddings and others, they mounted the wounded man on a horse and gave him the same treatment his partners in crime had received the day before.

J. L. Edwards was sheriff of Pawnee County but he was in Pawnee City, the county seat, at the time of the lynching and didn't hear about it until it was all done. He did launch an investigation to find the men responsible for the lynchings, and it began to look as if the affair was not at an end.

Several of the people who were considered models of respectability simply decided to move to greener pastures in other areas. The investigation was soon dropped. Some thought that if the law punished all who had a part in the lynching, Pawnee County might soon be depopulated. It was somewhat depopulated of Jayhawkers after the lynchings.

It wasn't easy living as a Jayhawker, renegade or not, in those days.

Stage Driver Killing— York County 1865

In 1864 Jack Smith established a ranch along the southern boundary of what would become York County. It would be six years before the county was officially organized. Smith's reason for starting his ranch there was to serve as a stopping place for those traveling the Nebraska City cut-off, which was many miles shorter than the ox-bow trail that followed the long loup of the Platte River. The Nebraska City cut-off traveled from Nebraska City to Fort Kearny in almost a straight line, part of the time following the West Fork of the Big Blue River.

The first murder in what would be York County took place at the Smith ranch. The ranch served as a place where travelers could get food and other supplies that they might need. The stage coaches also traveled this route.

It was a stage driver who created the trouble at the Smith ranch. He had gotten his hands on some home-made liquor, commonly called "Pioneer whiskey," and was looking for trouble. While the stage was stopped at the ranch and the passengers were being fed, the stage driver, letting the whiskey drive him, became very abusive and tried to pick a quarrel with Jack Smith.

Smith attempted to ignore him but the driver was not going to be ignored. So Smith tried to shut him up. The driver only became more incensed and yelled that he was going to shoot Smith.

He went outside to the coach and got his revolver. Smith saw what he was up to but still hardly believed he would do what he said. The driver came back to the house and when Smith stepped into the doorway, he pulled up his gun, aiming directly at Smith. His intentions were clear.

Smith had a gun and he promptly used it, shooting the driver right in the forehead. It was the first death in York County and the first burial. All the witnesses agreed that the stage driver had asked for what he got. Jack Smith was exonerated.

Horse Thieves—Merrick County 1866

Some places record murders in their early history and some seem to have a concentration of horse thieves. Merrick County, east of Grand Island, swarmed with the latter.

A man named Wood owned a fine team of mules and he started to Omaha for some special supplies, driving the mules. Shortly after leaving home, he came across two Irishmen who were afoot and were asking for a ride. Wood accommodated them and they became quite friendly. At Brewer's Ranch, they stopped for the night. The inn was crowded with workers cutting ties for the Union Pacific Railroad building to the west. The Irishmen said they would just roll up in their blankets outside.

Wood rose early the next morning to get a good start on his journey. But he discovered that the Irishmen had risen earlier. His mules were gone as was at least one saddle and bridle from the Brewer barn. The thieves had left tracks across some plowed ground, showing where they had departed the scene, going back to the northwest.

Wood sent telegrams to stations to the west to watch for the thieves and his mules.

One of the early stores in Chapman
Nebraska, Our Towns

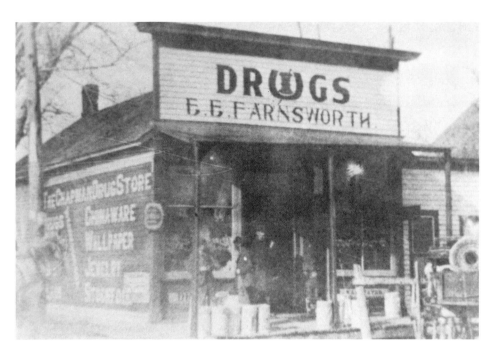

Silver Creek, about 1877
Nebraska, Our Towns

It was four days before any trace of the thieves was found. Then it was a loose mule that wandered into Wood River, west of Grand Island, that brought out the thieves. The sheriff took up the mule and when an Irishman came into town looking for a mule that had wandered away from his camp, the Irishman was arrested.

The Irishman refused to tell where his partner was until some loose talk about some cottonwood trees and short ropes untied his tongue. The other Irishman was arrested and the mules returned to Wood. The Irishmen were not hanged but were taken to the Douglas County jail, from which they escaped.

German Thief—Merrick County   1866

A few days after the Irishmen escaped, a tramp came along the river and stole a horse one night belonging to John Kyes. The thief, a German, headed for the river and crossed it. But he hit quicksand and had a struggle to get through. On the south bank, a freighter was camped. He heard the noise made by the thief and his horse, and went to the river bank to see what it was. At two o'clock in the morning, it seemed to the freighter that the man could hardly be coming over for a friendly visit. The thief crawled out of the river to face the freighter's gun. He was sullen and abusive when questioned about his reason for crossing the river in the middle of the night.

The freighter tied up the man and took him downstream at daylight to the J.T. Biggs ranch where Biggs recognized the horse as one belonging to John Kyes. So the thief was held until Kyes and a couple of "regulators" came to claim Kyes' horse.

The German was just as abusive to the three men as he had been to the freighter and wouldn't go with them to the sheriff. So they tied him to the tail of the horse he had stolen and they crossed the river, the horse swimming and dragging the thief along behind.

Once on the north shore, the three men held a conference to decide what to do with the German. He raved and swore at them and it solidified their decision. They put him on the stolen horse and tied him there, then headed into the wooded area nearby. Horse stealing was a hanging offense, they knew, and they decided they would mete out the penalty without listening to any more abuse from the thief.

The first rope they used broke the minute the German's bulk hit the end. But they had another rope and this one didn't break.

Shortly after this, another tragic incident

Sod house of the Knapp family; it was Palmer's first post office, Merrick County

Nebraska, Our Towns

took place in the county. John Vieregg and Claus Gottesh went hunting along the Loup River. They took Gottesh's son and a boy who worked for them. Toward evening the two men went to the river to hunt ducks, leaving the two boys with the team and wagon. When they returned, the found the two boys dead, shot in the blankets where they had gone to sleep. The horses were gone. They laid the blame on Indians but they had no proof that it wasn't a white thief who had committed the murders.

For a year or two, it seemed hardly safe either to own or steal a horse in Merrick County.

Ransel Grant Murder— Columbus, Platte County   January 1867

Ransel B. Grant and Robert Wilson were hauling wood for the Union Pacific Railroad that cold January in 1867. Wilson accused Grant of taking some wood from his pile. Grant denied it but he knew his denial meant nothing to Wilson.

It was common knowledge around the railroad camp that Wilson was a very quarrelsome man. It was rumored that he'd been in trouble before and had bought his way out of trouble with the law. This was not the first time that Wilson had quarreled with Grant, usually over something as silly as the accusation of taking some of Wilson's wood pile. So Grant didn't even bother to reply but kept loading his wagon.

Wilson raved for a moment then walked toward Grant. Too late, Grant realized that Wilson was angrier than usual. He whirled to meet him and it was then that Wilson deliberately shot Grant in the chest. It was the last thing Grant ever knew.

Wilson turned and walked to the store operated by John Rickly. Rickly was the man that both Wilson and Grant worked for. He marched into the store, and found Rickly settling an account with a customer. Wilson simply walked up to Rickly and told him flatly that he had just killed a man and he demanded that Rickly take him to Omaha to settle up. He said that he had seventeen hundred dollars and four wagons and four yokes of oxen.

Rickly turned from his customer to stare at his employee, wanting to know what his money had to do with what he had done. Wilson said he had killed a man in Indiana. He's had fourteen hundred dollars then and that had cleared him of any charge.

Rickly didn't believe Wilson at first. But Wilson insisted he wanted to go to Omaha; he didn't want to be tried here. Rickly took Wilson to an empty store room and locked him and his pet bulldog in the room then went to find Sheriff John Browner.

Browner went with Rickly to the store and got Wilson. Then they had Wilson show them where Grant was. Wilson took them to the site of the murder. They loaded the body in the wagon and Wilson stared at it in satisfaction. Rickly reported that he actually shook his fist at the corpse.

Ransel's brother, George Grant, heard about the murder that afternoon and he started stirring up public opinion for action against Wilson. Grant bought some rope and made a coil of it around his body and marched around town, calling for everyone to help him avenge his brother. Taking his campaign one step farther, he wrote what he called a death warrant and circulated it among his neighbors and friends to be signed. This "warrant" said something for the effectiveness of the law at that early stage of settlement in that area. The warrant read:

Columbus, Nebraska Territory, January 16, 1867

We, the undersigned, citizens of Columbus and vicinity, having become duly informed of all the circumstances connecting with the shooting of Ransel B. Grant by a person calling himself Robert Wilson, and being fully satisfied that the murder was without provocation and brutal in its character; and knowing the uncertainty of the law in this territory; and there being no safe place of confinement in the county; therefore, for these reasons and others which might be mentioned, we are firmly of the opinion that justice requires that the said Robert Wilson be executed without delay.

A coroner's inquest late that afternoon was held before Justice Hudson, and the trial was set for the next morning. The trial didn't come off until the next afternoon, and it was held before Justice Hudson, too.

That extra time gave George Grant time to circulate his petition and gather more signatures. There were many signatures on the "death warrant" and most of those men were present for the trial. Wilson was trembling when he saw the men. He had offered five hundred dollars to Hudson if he would let him "slope" out of the country. He upped the amount, but Hudson would not be bought off. He knew about the "warrant" circulating and he could sense the mood of the men who had signed it.

The trial was brief and the decision was to hold Robert Wilson for trial at the next general session of the court at Columbus. The fact that Justice Hudson had decreed that Wilson must be held for trial for murder was all the watchers needed.

The men surged forward and Wilson, seeing what was coming, tried to break away from the sheriff. Justice Hudson leaped forward to help block the men from getting to Wilson. He got jerked savagely away for his trouble. The sheriff was shoved aside and the men leaped on Wilson before he could reach the back door and escape. Wilson's dream of buying himself out of his troubles vanished.

Deputy Sheriff Wash Fulton joined the attempt to rescue the prisoner, but he was brushed rudely aside as had been the sheriff and the justice. Someone threw a rope over Wilson and he was dragged from the hall and down the street toward a tree a few rods southeast of the courtroom.

Just outside the justice's office, Wilson lost his hat, and his bulldog sat down beside the hat and stayed there for two or three days, not allowing anyone to get near that hat; not even a team of horses.

As they threw the rope over the limb of the tree, Wilson begged for the men to give him a chance. But they were recalling his confession of at least two murders, and his blatant attempt to buy his way to freedom. They also recalled that he had threatened several different workers who had crossed him, and they were convinced that the world would be better off without him. They gave the rope a quick jerk and left him dangling in the air.

After they were sure he was dead, they took the body down and, still in a vengeful mood, they dragged it down to the Loup River, cut a hole in the ice, and shoved the corpse through the hole head first. It was the last anyone ever saw of the murderer, Robert Wilson.

They took the money that Wilson had and gave it to Ransel Grant's widow and any personal property they found was left to be divided among the lawyers who attempted to defend him.

Clother Hotel, built in 1869. The rig in front met travelers at the depot.
Courtesy Nebraska State Historical Society

Scott Keysinger Murder— Otoe County 1867

On Saturday, January 26, 1867, several men were in the OK Saloon in Nebraska City. Apparently there had been some hot words exchanged between Scott Keysinger and George Karness. None of those questioned later seemed to recall anything particularly vehement between the two.

Several of the men started to leave the saloon. Jonathan Karness and Nicholas Ryan were among those leaving with Scott Keysinger. As Keysinger passed through the door, George Karness struck him over the head with his gun. The blow didn't knock Keysinger down and he wheeled on Karness with a knife. He swung at his assailant but the knife blade glanced off Karness, doing very little damage.

Karness then fired point blank at Keysinger, the bullet hitting him in the back as he was turned after swinging the knife. The bullet did not hit the heart but it did cut two arteries.

Men swarmed around to do what they could for Keysinger. Keysinger, however, broke away and ran back into the saloon, yelling that he had been shot. Dr. Livingstone was called immediately, but there was little he could do. The severed arteries spurted blood until Keysinger died about forty minutes later.

George Karness had disappeared immediately after he shot Keysinger. Jonathan Karness and Nicholas Ryan were still there and were arrested, since they had both been in George Karness' party.

Then the men started out to find George Karness, who had done the actual shooting. Near Karness' house, they found him. He was returning to the saloon to see what had happened after he left.

Deputy Sheriff Fairfield was in the crowd of men now, and he arrested George Karness and took him to jail. The coroner's jury handed down the verdict that Scott Keysinger died from a gunshot fired by George Karness. So George was charged with the murder and lodged in jail to await trail. Jonathan Karness and Nicholas Ryan were released because there was no evidence they were implicated in any way in the killing.

Territorial days were winding down. Nebraska would soon be a state. Would statehood bring more law and order?

BIBLIOGRAPHY

BOOKS

Andreas, A. T. *History of Nebraska*. Chicago: Western History Collection, 1882.

Sheldon, Addison E. *History and Stories of Nebraska*. Chicago: University Publishing Co., 1913.

BULLETINS

Nebraska Games and Parks Commission. *Rock Creek Station*.

State Historical Park Bulletin. *Rock Creek Station*.

NEWSPAPERS

Cumings City News. June 19, 1858.

Falls City Broad Ax. August 20, 1861.

Nebraska Advertiser, Brownville. September 6, 1857; January 30, 1859; August 22, 1863; May 2, 1864; September 1, 1864.

Nebraska City News. August 13, 1859; October 1, 1859; February 3, 1865; February 1, 1867.

Nebraska Herald, Plattsmouth. January 19, 1860.

Nebraska Inquirer. October 6, 1859.

Nemaha City Herald. April 19, 1860.

Omaha Nebraskan. August 29, 1860; September 20, 1860.

III

GROWING PAINS

1867–1900

Growing Pains

Growing from a territory to a state didn't guarantee a graduation from territorial lawlessness to statehood perfection. Nebraska brought into statehood much of the territorial rowdiness that had ruled the area through the previous years.

Becoming a state meant more people and more opportunity for the evil-minded to cheat, steal, even kill. And with the great expanse to the west that was included in the boundaries of the state, there were more places to hide and less chance of being apprehended for a criminal act. Many counties in the west end of the state not only had their own territory to govern, but often they were given jurisdiction over the land to their west between them and the state line. Until the counties that had been marked off in those areas accumulated enough people to organize their own governments, the people there had to look to the county to the east for their government and their protection.

As each new county learned to govern itself, it was usually tested by those who lived by their own laws and defied rules and regulations.

Those early years of statehood, from 1867 to 1900, were fraught with growing pains, some of which left scares; but Nebraska came through into the next century stronger and surer of itself because of the lessons it had learned.

Davis Killing—Douglas County   1869

In late October, 1869, the court in Omaha had to make a decision on what constituted justifiable homicide. The man on trial was William Broaddus. Just a couple of days before he had committed the murder, his victim, George Davis, had coaxed Broaddus's eight-year-old daughter into the cellar of a vacant house near the Metropolitan Hotel and there mistreated her.

When Broaddus found out about it, he was ready to kill. He armed himself and went out in search of Davis. He found him in the doorway of his home. He invited Davis to his place to talk about a deal. Davis, not suspecting that Broaddus knew what had happened, followed him to Broaddus's home. Once inside the house, Broaddus asked his daughter if this was the man who had hurt her. She said, "Yes. Make him go away."

Broaddus drew his pistol and shot Davis where he stood. Davis screamed and ran from the house. Reaching the street, he ran to the doorway of the corner drug store and there he collapsed and died.

Broaddus walked to the police station as soon as he had shot Davis and turned himself in. He was brought to trial. Many thought he should be commended for defending his family; others thought that murder under any provocation should be punished. The courtroom was filled with people who had feelings ranging from a hope that Broaddus would be set free to those who thought he should be hanged for murder.

The jury brought in a verdict of guilty. The judge set sentence at just five years in the penitentiary.

Gallon Murder—Dodge County   1869

George and Daniel Gallon drove down from West Point to Fremont on the 16th of November, 1869, and went to the St. Charles Hotel. They put up their team in the

1870 view of West Point

Nebraska, Our Towns

adjoining livery stable for feed while they went into the hotel bar.

George went out to settle their feed bill with the owner, John H. Smith. Smith asked what Gallon considered an enormous price for the feed bill. They got into an argument and it got hotter by the minute.

Daniel Gallon came out to see what was holding up his brother and he found Smith chasing George with an uplifted neckyoke. There was no doubt in Daniel's mind that Smith intended to use the neckyoke. He called a halt to everything and talked the two men into settling their differences without violence.

They both agreed, Smith reluctantly. However, the feed bill still had to be settled. When it was brought up, Smith suddenly lunged at George and hit him over the head with the neckyoke. George was knocked off his feet. Before Daniel could interfere again, Smith hit George another terrific blow to the head, crushing his skull. George died before morning.

Smith was arrested and charged with murder. His trial was held at the next term of court, and he was found guilty and sentenced to ten years in the penitentiary.

The next night after the trial, Smith escaped from jail and no one in Dodge County ever saw him again.

Dunn Murder—Dixon County   1870

The only true justice, as most early settlers saw it, was justice meted out quickly and effectively. That was their approach to the murder of a kindly old man named Dunn who had just crossed the Missouri River from Iowa into Dixon County. It was July, and Matthew Miller saw him and decided he surely had some money on him.

Ponca Agency Government School, 1904
Courtesy Nebraska State Historical Society

Miller needed money desperately. He waited until Dunn had gone into a grove along the river near Ponca and followed him. There, instead of just holding up the man, Miller killed him and took all the money he had.

When Mr. Dunn's body was found, suspicious centered on Matt Miller because he'd been seen near the grove. He was arrested and brought to trial before a jury of the people on hand. The jury was not limited to twelve men but included everyone present to hear the evidence. A minister, Reverend Beardshear, was put in charge of the proceedings.

With the evidence piling up against him,

Miller confessed his crime. A vote of all those present was taken to decide his fate. The vote was almost unanimous. He should die for what he had done. A life for a life was their definition of true justice.

Not having any heavy lumber to build a scaffold, they found three long slim poles that they called scantlings, too weak to hold much alone but, bound together at one end like a tripod, they were strong enough to serve as a gallows. They erected the scantlings near the school house and hanged Miller there that day, July 23, 1870. Swift and sure. That was the settlers' definition of true justice.

Neligh from Academy Hill, 1886
Nebraska, Our Towns

Fletcher Murder— Antelope County   1871

The first murder in Antelope County occurred just about the time that the county itself was organized. That was in the spring of 1871.

R.A. Rollins had just taken his homestead and built his house on it. A neighbor, J.P. Fletcher, frequently traveled a road that ran within a few feet of Rollins' new house. When the road was first made, the land had been unclaimed. But now Rollins didn't want Fletcher to use the road that came so close to his house.

It became a hot argument every time Fletcher drove by. Rollins couldn't see why Fletcher couldn't make new tracks a little farther from the house. Fletcher thought that the road had been there before Rollins had built his house so the road took precedent. Rollins could have built his house a little farther from the road.

The argument got hotter each time it was renewed. Rollins had hired a man named Frank Cottle to help him break the sod. Cottle got into the argument occasionally, always on the side of Rollins.

It seemed like a stalemate. Rollins continued to insist that Fletcher move his road over a little. Fletcher was stubborn and had no intention of letting anybody tell him where he could drive.

The argument came to a head suddenly one day when neither Fletcher nor Rollins expected it. Cottle, probably thinking he was helping the man he was working for, took a hand in the argument and he had a gun. Things erupted in a flurry of action. When it was over, J.P. Fletcher was dead. Rollins had a hole through his ear.

Cottle was arrested and found guilty of killing Fletcher. His sentence, however, was only six months in prison. Even that was cut in half and after three months, he was released.

Very early picture of
Burnett-Tilden
Nebraska, Our Towns

Stege Stage in front of Aerdome Theatre. The stage took people to hotels.
Nebraska, Our Towns

Cameron Murder—Gage County   1872

In April of 1872, two men, the best of friends, left Grasshopper Falls, Kansas, to work on a railroad that was being built in southeastern Nebraska. John Cameron was the younger of the two but he owned a good team and wagon. Jackson Marion bought the outfit from him, promising to pay Cameron installments after they arrived on the railroad job in Nebraska. Marion gave Cameron thirty dollars and a note for the rest.

It took them almost a month to reach Jack Marion's mother-in-law's place on Wildcat Creek in southwestern Gage County. After staying there three or four days they moved on toward their summer job. From there, the facts are rather obscure. Jack Marion returned to his mother-in-law's place a few days after the pair left. He was alone now, but he had the team and wagon he had bought from Cameron and the camping equipment the two men had taken. He said that John Cameron had decided to go back to Kansas and had struck out alone.

Marion stayed with his mother-in-law for a few days, then he disappeared. Nobody knew or cared where he had gone.

It was a year later that a skeleton was found along the banks of a creek not far from the home of Mrs. Warren, Marion's mother-in-law. The skeleton had three bullet holes in the skull and there was enough of the clothing left to identify the clothes as belonging to John Cameron. An inquest was held, and the coroner's jury reached the decision that John Cameron had met his death at the hands of his companion, Jackson Marion.

But Marion had gone and nobody had any idea where he was. Investigation showed that Cameron hadn't been seen anywhere in

Beatrice in 1860

Courtesy Nebraska State Historical Society

Kansas, either, after he left with Marion for the railroad job. Everyone was convinced that the inquest had reached the right conclusion. But there could be no punishment handed out for the murder because Jack Marion had disappeared.

Over ten years after the murder, in December, 1882, Sheriff Herron of Gage County heard that Jackson Marion was in jail in a Kansas town near the Indian Territory, charged with larceny. Sheriff Herron went to the little Kansas town and got Marion and brought him back to Beatrice. Marion did not plead guilty to the murder of his friend, but he was indicted for murder, anyway.

The case came up in district court in May, 1883. It was a case that held the interest of the surrounding county. There were people living in Kansas where the two had left together, and some who had seen them while near Beatrice on their way through the country. These were brought in as witnesses. Cameron's skeleton, and the clothing still intact after he had been found, was exhumed from the cemetery back in Iowa where it had been buried and brought to Beatrice for the trial.

The trial lasted several days. The jury found Jack Marion guilty, and the judge sentenced him to hang in September, 1883. The defense counsel asked for a new trial on grounds that the crime had taken place on reservation land. The Supreme Court turned down the request. However, it granted a new trial based on the fact that, back in 1872 when the murder was committed, juries not only decided the guilt or innocence of a person on trial but also decreed the penalty. Since the judge had set this punishment, Marion should get a new trial under the conditions that existed when the crime was committed. The jury must set the penalty.

On this small variance, Marion was granted a new trial. Marion went back to the county jail to await that trial. He was there almost two years before the second trial reached the docket in April, 1885.

The same witnesses appeared again and gave the same testimony. One man, Jacob Worley from Kansas, testified that he knew that Marion had bought a team and wagon from Cameron for two hundred and twenty-five dollars, paying Cameron thirty dollars and giving him a note for the balance. He also bought a wagon from Cameron for ninety dollars. They had left for their job in that wagon.

The jury reached the same decision as the previous jury had, and this time it recommended the punishment, too: death by hanging. The sentence was to be carried out on June 26, 1885.

The Supreme Court was asked to review the case, and that called for another postponement of the penalty. When the Supreme Court ruled that the penalty should not be changed, the new date for the execution was set for March 11, 1887.

By that time, public sentiment had brought about other complications. Almost one thousand letters flooded Governor Thayer's office, and he ordered a stay of execution until he could review these petitions for a commutation of the death penalty to life imprisonment. After consideration, the governor refused to interfere with the orders of the district court, and the execution date was set for a fourth time. It was to be March 25, 1887.

This time the decree was carried out. Jackson Marion never confessed to the crime. His biggest complaint was that so many murderers escaped execution even when there were eye witnesses to the deed, but he was convicted on circumstantial evidence and was going to have to pay with his life. There was little doubt in the minds of those who had witnessed the trial that the verdict was correct. Marion's hanging was the only legal execution in Gage County.

Nebraska Governor John M. Thayer
Courtesy Nebraska State Historical Society

There were some strange repercussions that arose long after the sentence had been carried out. For instance, in August of 1891, a story burst on the pages of the Beatrice paper that John Cameron had been found alive. That would mean that Jackson Marion had been executed for a murder that never happened. It became the talk of the territory. Some were convinced, but many were not.

It was William Wymore, Jack Marion's uncle, who uncovered the story. He reported to the *Beatrice Daily Express* that he had found and talked to John Cameron not long before. In his story, he said that he had heard that Cameron was in southwestern Kansas over a year before. He had spent a lot of time trying to find him.

Then just a couple of weeks before he reported to the *Express*, he heard that he was in LaCrosse, Kansas, northwest of Great Bend. After contacting him by letter, Wymore had convinced Cameron to meet him near LaCrosse. Wymore had gone there and talked with Cameron. Of course, the *Express* wanted to know if Wymore was certain in was Cameron. He was positive.

Then the question came as to where Cameron had been over those nineteen years since he and Marion had parted company. Wymore said Cameron had told him he had gone directly to Mexico and worked in the mines there for four years, then had gone up into California and on to Alaska. He had just returned from there a year or two before. He had worked in the mines in Colorado until he came to Kansas. He hadn't heard about the trouble his friend, Jack Marion, had been in until about a year ago. Wymore said Cameron still had the note Marion had given him for the team and wagon.

Wymore said Cameron told that he had left because he was afraid of a paternity suit if he stayed around. He said he traded his clothes to an Indian for some blankets shortly after he left Marion.

Wymore said that explained the skeleton's clothes. They had been found on the Otoe Indian Reservation. The story received some credibility among the citizens, but not all were convinced. The story left room for many questions and not a few arguments.'

There is one other postscript to this story. A pardon for Jackson Marion was granted in December, 1986, to become effective on March 25, 1987, the one hundredth anniversary of Marion's execution.

Day Murder—Fillmore County 1872

Orlando Porter had come from Ohio and taken a homestead east of Geneva. He had turned the land into a good farm. George A.

Day had taken a homestead later near Porter. Day had yet to bring his wife and family to the homestead and, in the meantime, was boarding with the Porters.

Day was to help Porter with the farm work to pay for his board and room but on many days, the boarder complained of not feeling well and had stayed at the house.

On one such day, Porter was working in the hay field with a neighbor. The neighbor reluctantly told him what he had heard rumored, and what he himself suspected; that Day was becoming very familiar with Porter's wife. Porter went home immediately.

Day was not there at the time, although he had complained of not feeling well enough to work that day. Porter sat down with his wife and demanded an explanation. She finally confessed that it was true. Porter was furious and swore that he would kill Day.

Just then Porter looked out the window and saw his boarder riding into the yard on a horse he had borrowed from Porter. Grabbing a loaded gun, he pointed the muzzle through the open window and fired. Day rolled off the horse, dead before he hit the ground.

Porter was charged with murder and held for trial. The fall term of court was in November, 1872, and Porter was convicted of manslaughter. Considering the provocation, the judge sentenced him to just one year in the penitentiary. The jury later signed a petition asking for his pardon. Porter did serve only a few months and then he was released. He immediately took his wife and went back to Ohio where he had come from.

Easter Blizzard—Howard County   1873

Nebraska is known for two kinds of killer storms, blizzards and tornadoes. The blizzard on Easter Sunday, April 13, 1873, was particularly bad because it came late in the season for a blizzard and people coming from the east had never experienced a bad blizzard and just didn't know how to prepare for one.

This blizzard started as so many bad storms do, with a cold rain. About dark, the wind switched to the northwest and the rain became sleet, that stung like bird shot, then fine snow. The wind turned bitter cold and sucked the breath right out of a man's lungs.

Livestock that had been soaked by the rain during the day now chilled, and some settlers lost every head of their livestock—cows, horses, and chickens. Some settlers had built sheds for their cattle, but the cattle kept milling around in the sheds to stay on top of the snow that was whipping in through the door until their backs hit the roofs as they trampled the snow underfoot. Some sheds lost their roofs.

In Howard County, the Cooper family was caught completely by surprise. Mr. Cooper and his son had gone to Grand Island before the rain, and had decided to wait until the rain was over before going home. They were caught in town by the blizzard.

Back at the homestead, not far from St. Paul, Mrs. Cooper and the two daughters, Lizzie and Emma, were also caught unprepared. They didn't have much fuel in the house, but the girls kept the house as warm as they could. Their mother was sick in bed.

A particularly strong blast of wind slammed the door open and scattered coals out of the fireplace. Little fires sprang up but the snow kept them from becoming dangerous. Then another blast lifted the roof off the house. All the girls could do then was pile every blanket and tick they had on the bed and climb under them, one of each side of their mother, trying to keep her warm.

By morning, the blizzard was still raging. The girls knew they had to get help or their mother would not survive. So they wrapped their mother in all the blankets they had, put on their coats and ventured out into the

Old Cotesfield School, 1905

Nebraska, Our Towns

storm, hoping to reach a neighbor who could help them.

They had barely fought their way through the snow packed doorway before they were lost. They had never known wind so hard but they pressed on, trying to follow the road that ran close to their house. That road ran from Coatsfield to St. Paul. Lizzie had taught a term of school in St. Paul and she felt she could find her way around even in a storm. But there was no direction in this storm. The wind was from the northwest, they thought, and they had to keep their backs to it in order to breathe.

They soon became very tired fighting their way through the drifts they couldn't even see. By nightfall they were so tired they could barely move. Lizzie was in worse shape than Emma. The two snuggled down close together, letting the snow pile over them. It seemed to Emma that it was warmer that way. They were out of that biting wind.

They got out of the snow the next morning and began struggling on, no longer having any idea where they were or where they were going. Lizzie was completely exhausted. In spite of Emma's encouragement, Lizzie sank into the snow and Emma couldn't get her up.

The snow was decreasing but the wind still howled like a banshee. Emma soon

A blizzard that paralyzed most of
Nebraska
Nebraska, Our Towns

Crew cuts through snow drifts
Nebraska, Our Towns

realized that Lizzie was dead. She had to
struggle on. She moved ahead, not really
aware of anything except that she had to
keep moving. Finally the snow stopped. Only
a ground blizzard continued.

Emma would have died in a short time if
W.P. Wyman hadn't discovered her crawling
past his house on her hands and knees. She'd

had no idea she was close to a house. Wyman
took her into the house where he and his wife
slowly revived her. When she was able to
talk, she told them about her sister and about
her mother alone back in what was left of the
Cooper house.

Wyman quickly got some men and they
fought their way through the drifts to the
Cooper house. They found no one in the
house and they began a search. They found
Mrs. Cooper some distance from the house,
frozen. They speculated that she had become
worried about her daughters and had gone
out to look for them.

Others died in that storm, too. Dillon
Haworth had settled on Spring Creek which
ran into the main Loup River. He had a wife
and two children. They apparently became
frantic when the storm continued beyond
their fuel supply and they started out to go to
a neighbor's pace. They were found a day
after the storm had blown itself out. Only the
smallest child, one and a half years old,
survived. She was clutched to her dead
mother's breast when they found the family.

Blizzards on the Nebraska plains and

House almost buried in snow
Courtesy Ferne Coxbill

prairies could be deadly to the uninitiated. And all the early settlers were among the uninitiated. Only experience could make survivors of those pioneers. It was an Easter none of the survivors would ever forget.

Hondesheld Poisoning— Saline County 1874

The final punishment for murder did not always end at the short end of a rope. An example of that occurred in 1874 in Saline County. A couple named Hondesheld lived on a farm about six miles northwest of Crete. They quarreled a lot, and it finally reached the point where Mrs. Hondesheld encouraged her husband to find a place to live in town. Since she was the dominant partner in the marriage, he packed his things and moved into Crete. But he still went out almost daily to work on the farm.

On occasion his wife would prepare something for his lunch. It added to the small lunch that he brought out from town. On one occasion, she gave him a generous piece of

First building in St. Paul, built in 1871
Nebraska, Our Towns

pie to finish off his lunch. He loved pie and appreciated the gift.

They found him in the wagon that afternoon dead. Half of the piece of pie was still uneaten. The officer took the pie to town and had it analyzed. It was very heavily laced with strychnine. Mrs. Hondesheld was arrested and taken to jail.

The county seat in 1874 was at Pleasant Hill, south and a little west of Crete, so Mrs. Hondesheld was put in the jail there and held for trial. The trial ended in a hung jury, so she was put back in jail to await a new trial.

Three men were in the jail one night charged with minor offenses. Two of them were not willing to wait until the sheriff released them at the end of their short sentences, and decided to break out. They had some kindling and matches, so they set a fire to burn the lock off the cell door.

The problem was that the lock did not burn, and the inmates could not escape the fire that consumed the jail. All four, including Mrs. Hondesheld, died in the blaze. As for Mrs. Hondesheld, most people were convinced that she was guilty of killing her husband and felt that she got her just desserts; something the law might not have given her.

Vroman Murder— Minden, Kearney County   1875

At a farm near Minden, trouble oozed into the air like spring water rising in a bog. A man named Williams owned the farm and he had a family named Vroman living with him. There was a personality clash that should have resulted in one family moving out, but it didn't.

The animosity exploded into a hot quarrel one day and Vroman and his nearly grown son won the argument. But still the Vromans stayed at the Williams farm.

A short time after the quarrel, Williams'

driving team died. Since both horses died at the same time, Williams was convinced that Vroman had poisoned them. He accused the Vromans of killing his horses. Since he couldn't prove it, there was nothing more he could do. But the Vromans moved to another house only a short distance from the Williams farm.

It wasn't long after that when Williams' riding pony got loose and wandered over close to the place where Vroman now lived. Vroman took up the pony and sent word to Williams that he could get his pony back by paying for the feed Vroman had given it.

Williams went after his pony, but he was in no mood to pay the Vromans for any feed. The confrontation was brief. Williams had his shotgun with him and when the argument got hot, he shot both Vrroman and his son.

Mrs. Vroman was at the house a few dozen yards away and saw what had happened. She rushed down to the barn and found her husband and son dead. Williams and his pony were gone.

Williams was arrested and his trial was scheduled in Minden, but feeling was so strong there that the defense asked for a change of venue, and the trial was shifted to Hastings in Adams County. There Williams was convicted and sentenced to ten years in the penitentiary.

Clough Murder—Seward County   1876

Nathan Clough rode his prize black stallion into Seward the afternoon of April 30, 1876. He often rode into Seward and spent the night because his brother, Warren, and his wife owned and operated a hotel in Seward called the Blue Valley House. Nathan and Warren were on the best of terms in spite of the fact that Warren was considered wealthy, while Nathan was a man of only moderate means.

Town of Seward, 1900

Nathan never took a room in Warren's hotel because he wanted to stay close to his valuable stallion. This night, like all nights on previous visits, Nathan put his stallion in the hotel stable then climbed into the loft directly above the stallion's stall and made his bed in the hay.

Nathan and Warren looked quite a bit alike. Both were tall and considered by most to be two of the more handsome men around. Warren didn't even invite Nathan to sleep inside the hotel, knowing he would never allow himself to be that far from his prize stallion.

When morning came, Warren expected Nathan to come in for breakfast. When he didn't show up on time, he went outside, found the hostler who cared for the horses of overnight guests at the hotel, and asked him about Nathan. The hostler said that Nathan apparently was sleeping late. He hadn't heard any sound from him when he had gone in to give the horses their morning hay and grain.

Warren went on to the stable and called for Nathan. Getting no answer, he climbed into the loft and found Nathan wrapped tightly in his blankets and a buffalo robe. It had been chilly the night before. But Warren was stunned by the sight of Nathan's forehead split open by an ax. Blood had run down his face and dropped through the loft floor onto the mane on his stallion.

Warren called the sheriff and a quick investigation was made. They found no money on Nathan. Warren said that Nathan had received a thousand dollars recently from an estate in Appanose County, Iowa, and he had told Warren that he had spent three hundred dollars of it paying his bills. There was no money to be found on Nathan. Warren was sure he'd had the seven hundred dollars with him the night before.

The sheriff began inquiring as to who could have known that Nathan had money with him. No one, it seemed, had known anything about Nathan's inheritance but

Warren. Further investigation turned up nothing else and suspicion pointed toward Warren. In spite of Warren's denial, the sheriff arrested Warren on a charge of murdering his brother.

Warren was put in jail. Those who knew Warren were shocked and almost all were convinced that arresting him was a big mistake. Then as Nathan's affairs were beginning to be cleared up, another bit of evidence popped up that put Warren in a worse light. Nathan had recently separated from his wife and had made a new will. He left only a little of his wealth to his wife (they were not divorced) and all the rest went to Warren. It gave the prosecution more ammunition to use at the trial. Not only was the seven hundred dollars missing and claimed by the prosecution to surely have been taken by Warren, but now Warren was to profit a great deal by his brother's death through the will that Nathan had recently made.

All of Warren's denials were shunted aside. He'd have his day in court to prove his innocence. Many of Warren's friends remained loyal; they were positive that he was innocent. But those who were not close to him were being swayed by the evidence, even though circumstantial, piling up against him.

The trial date approached but it quickly became evident that they would not be able to get an unprejudiced jury in Seward. Everyone had heard of the murder and almost everyone had made up his mind whether Warren was guilty or not. So the judge called for a change of venue. The trial was moved to York in Hamilton County, just to the west of Seward.

The trial date came. The judge was G.W. Post. The prosecution was headed by District Attorney M.B. Buse. Assisting him were Looley and Leese of Seward and William T. Scott of York.

Judge Oliver Perry Mason
Courtesy Nebraska State Historical Society

The defense was led by Judge Oliver Perry Mason, a very well known attorney in Nebraska. He was from Lincoln. He had an even larger battery of assistants than the prosecution had. The Norval Brothers of Seward were helping, as well as Judge Edward Bates and George B. France, both of York.

One hundred and twenty-one prospective jurors were called before twelve were selected. All the time new bits of circumstantial evidence piled up, until it appeared that even the great O.P. Mason couldn't free Warren Clough of the charge of murdering his brother.

The trial lasted for a month. The court room was filled to capacity almost every session. People came for miles, especially from Seward County, and many camped near York and hurried in each morning to get a seat in the court room. Passions were divided. There were those who declared that Warren Clough could not possibly be guilty of murder. Others looked at the evidence and were convinced that only Warren's hanging could clear the air of this foul crime.

The trial finally ended and the jury was instructed. They brought back a verdict of guilty of murder in the first degree. Some cheered; others groaned. Warren's friends would not believe he was guilty. O.P. Mason appealed the decision to the state supreme court. But that court did not change the verdict. Warren Clough was sentenced to die by hanging.

Since the trial had been held in Hamilton County, the sentence was to be carried out in York. The gallows were to be built in the court yard just a few yards from the jail cell where Warren Clough waited for his last day of life.

Warren's friends did not give up. They were not convinced that the circumstantial evidence was correct. They flooded the governor's desk with letters until he finally took notice, reviewed the case, and commuted the death sentence to life imprisonment. The hammers on the scaffold stopped. Warren cleared his ears of the dreadful beat, and he was transported to Lincoln to spend the rest of his life in prison there.

After he had been in prison for a while, Warren gave up ever seeing freedom again. His wife, according to the law, could and did divorce Warren, and took their son and moved to Oklahoma, far away from the stigma that had fallen on the family.

Then one day, fifteen long years after Warren Clough had been committed to the state penitentiary, a fellow prisoner named Jack Trent confessed on his death bed that he had used the ax on Nathan Clough and robbed him of the seven hundred dollars.

O.P. Mason immediately went to then-Governor Thayer and requested the release of Warren from prison. After hearing what had happened, the governor asked how long it would take to get him released from prison. Mason told him just as long as it would take the governor to sign the papers and put them in Mason's hand. Mason went personally to the prison and took Warren Clough out into freedom.

Warren was gray headed and stooped now, his health in bad shape. Free at last, he went back to Seward and York to see his friends, blaming no one for the circumstances that had sent him to prison. From York he went to Oklahoma to see his former wife and his son. He settled in Oklahoma and a few years later, his friends back in Nebraska received word that he had died. The prison bars had been taken away but his shattered life could not be put back together.

Hallowell—Murder and Lynching— Dawson County 1876

It wasn't exactly premeditated murder, but the warning had been issued well before the act was committed.

It was a bitter argument between Tom Hallowell and Julius Trackett. The homestead claim in question was about five miles from Plum Creek on Danielson Island. Hallowell was living on the claim but Trackett declared it was his land. Trackett got a writ of ejection to get Hallowell thrown off the land. Deputy Sheriff Charles Mayes was given the job of serving the paper.

Hallowell had threatened to shoot anyone who tried to evict him, so Mayes got two men, Julius Wien and R.S. Freeman, to go with him. On June 17, 1876, the three men rode from Plum Creek out to Danielson Island.

When Tom Hallowell saw them coming, he ran into the house, shutting the door and barring it. When the three reached the door and demanded that he let them in, Hallowell shouted that he would shoot the first man who came in.

Mayes was determined to do his duty and, with the aid of the two men with him, they broke down the door. Mayes charged through the door. Hallowell fired one barrel of his shotgun, killing Mayes instantly.

Wien and Freeman started in and Hallowell fired the other barrel. Wien was slightly injured, but it only enraged the little German and he leaped over Mayes' body into the house. Hallowell's gun was empty now and he threw it down and begged the two men not to shoot him.

Hallowell was handcuffed and R.C. Freeman took him to Plum Creek while Julius Wien stayed with the body of the deputy sheriff. A coroner's inquest was held and reached the only possible conclusion, death by gunshot at the hands of Thomas Hallowell.

Charles Mayes had been a very popular man in Plum Creek and there was quite a furor over his murder. Hallowell was not too well liked, anyway, and now he had reached the bottom of the scale with his actions of the day. Angry talk circulated over the town but no serious threats were made.

But about eleven o'clock that night, about twenty masked men moved quietly in around the courthouse. Only one man, C.J. Dilworth, the prosecuting attorney, seemed to suspect there might be something afoot and he went down to the courthouse a while before midnight. However, he was met by two masked men and politely informed that he wasn't needed there. He let the two men know that he thought he was needed. The two men didn't budge from their decision and finally prevailed on the attorney that he'd better not try to interfere.

The crowd of masked men closed in on the courthouse. The leader called for the guard to open the door. The guard shouted back that he didn't have the key. Not only that, the guard was locked inside the courthouse himself.

The men didn't hesitate. They had established their goal and they intended to reach it. They promptly battered down the door. Leaping inside, one man blew out the lamp while the others overwhelmed the guard. They tied the guard to a chair then anchored the chair to a bedpost. They blindfolded him then one man lit the lamp again.

The men forced the lock in the door leading to the jail cells and then got the keys and unlocked the cell where Hallowell was being held. Hallowell begged to be allowed to live; at least, one more day.

The men ignored his pleas. They were still moving quietly, methodically. There was none of the yelling and raving that so often associated men bent on righting a wrong. The town wasn't awakened by what was happening.

Hallowell was dragged from his cell, a rope placed around his neck, and then he was led around to the back of the courthouse. Iron stairs led up to the second floor courtroom. A sturdy iron railing rimmed the stairs and the landing at the top.

The end of the rope was fastened securely to the iron railing at the top and Hallowell was thrown over. The next morning the town found Hallowell hanging there, his feet a foot-and-a-half off the ground.

An attempt was made to find the men who had lynched Tom Hallowell but there were no clues, and the townspeople accepted the fact that justice had been meted out, whether legally or not.

Chapman Killing—
Loup City, Sherman County   1877

Total shock would probably best describe the paralysis that gripped the Sherman County seat town of Loup City one afternoon in late February in 1877.

Some men were lounging near the little grocery store in town when one of the men went into the store to buy some tea his wife had told him to get. While he was there, a young man named George McKellar came up, obviously in bad shape from too much liquor. Still no one gave it much thought. He'd been in this condition before.

Then Chapman, who had gone in for the tea, came out of the store. For no apparent reason, McKellar shot Chapman, who collapsed on the store's little porch.

Shock gripped the men. (Chapman was a man with no enemies, so far as his friends knew.) Then one man ran for the doctor to tend to Chapman; another went for the sheriff.

In the meantime, George McKellar tightened the cinch on his saddle as he would under ordinary circumstances, mounted his horse and rode out of town. Nobody could explain later whether it was shock that kept them from stopping McKellar or whether they were waiting for the sheriff to officially arrest the killer.

The doctor arrived and did what he could for Chapman, but he died in less than two days. The shock was gone from the town, but not the anger. Chapman had been well liked. The sheriff and other men searched the country for McKellar, but no sign of him was found. The sheriff offered a reward of $500 for his arrest. The search intensified but with no luck.

Then George McKellar's own father brought him in. George's only excuse for killing Chapman was that he was drunk. In today's court that might have been accepted as an excuse, but not back in the settlement days of the 1870s.

The trial was held in April of that year, less than two months after the murder. McKellar was found guilty and held fully

Rosseter House, Loup City, built in 1873
Nebraska, Our Towns

accountable for what he had done. It was his choice to get drunk; therefore, he was totally responsible for anything he did while drunk.

The judge sentenced him to the penitentiary for life. McKellar went to prison with little hope of getting out for a long time, if ever.

St. Louis Murder—Dodge County   1877

In 1877, Dr. St. Louis, a prominent physician in Fremont, committed suicide. But there is more to the story than that.

In May of that year, Mrs. St. Louis took sick and within two weeks she was dead. The doctor had obviously tried to save his wife but couldn't cure her stomach ailment.

There might not have been any question about her death if it had not been for the doctor's actions. Even when she was so seriously ill, the doctor was seen spending time with a Mrs. Bloomer. Mrs. Bloomer was a patient of Dr. St. Louis but many suspected that she was much more than a patient. Even on the morning after Mrs. St. Louis's death, Dr. St. Louis was seen going up the stairs to Mrs. Bloomer's abode.

The circumstances were so strange that some citizens insisted on an autopsy of Mrs. St. Louis. They were not surprised to find grains of arsenic in her stomach. Dr. St. Louis was arrested and charged with the murder of his wife. He emphatically denied it.

The circumstances being what they were, he was brought to trial. The doctor insisted that he was innocent of the charge. He and his wife had been very happy together; there were no grounds for the charge against him. As for the arsenic found in his wife's stomach, he said that one of the men conducting the autopsy was an enemy of his and very easily could have slipped the grains of arsenic into the stomach of the body.

The trial ended in a deadlock. A change of venue was granted and the new trial was conducted in Saunders County. Here Dr. St. Louis was found guilty and sentenced to be executed in April, 1879.

Dr. St. Louis never veered from his insistence that he was innocent and declared that they were preparing to kill an innocent man. Somehow, he got his hands on a small pistol and, on the morning of the scheduled execution, he shot himself in the head. Whether he shot an innocent man or a murderer was never determined to the complete satisfaction of some people of Fremont.

View of Wahoo in 1878
Courtesy Saunders County
Historical Society

Colby Murder—Furnas County 1877

A widow, Mrs. Colby, and a man who claimed to be her uncle, Willard Sawyer, came to Furnas County sometime after the county was organized and took adjoining homesteads; but they lived together in a one room house.

Log cabin built near Beaver City in 1872

Nebraska, Our Towns

For some time things went well, but then they began quarreling. One night, Sawyer wrote a letter stating the real situation. Mrs. Colby was a widow and Sawyer had left his family to live with her. Then they had come west and homesteaded. Now he intended to kill her, then commit suicide.

From the evidence they found the following afternoon when someone came to the cabin, they surmised that Sawyer had killed Mrs. Colby just as she was preparing for bed. Her body was partially undressed. There was evidence of a terrific struggle. Things were scattered everywhere. There was blood splattered over the floor and the bed. Sawyer had apparently accomplished his mission when he finally hit the woman just above the ear with a hammer, crushing her skull.

Then he had sat down and written another letter that told more of the story. A neighbor filled in the gap between the evening murder and the morning suicide. About eight that morning, Sawyer had appeared at the

neighbor's house and borrowed a shotgun. Taking it back to the cabin, he apparently had put the muzzle in his mouth and pulled the trigger. The blast tore off the side of his face but didn't kill him instantly. He died that evening, thus saving the county an expensive murder trial.

Kotiza Murder—Douglas County 1878

Sometimes a murder is committed for which there seems to be little or no motive. On September 1, 1878, there was a ball at Bohemian Gardens. There was the usual crowd but there were five young men who were a little too boisterous. Perhaps Johnny Barleycorn might have had something to do with that. The five were Austin Kotiza, Anton Moestrick, George Rider, Patrick Quinlan, and John Lewis.

View of Omaha, looking toward Capitol Hill, 1870s

Courtesy Douglas County Historical Society

They got into a bit of an argument on the dance floor. Quinlan found a stick and was standing back from the others and Moestrick accused him of planning an assault on him. Quinlan denied it. An argument erupted and the five went outside. A crowd followed, the way crowds always gather around a fight.

It was quite a fight until one man yelled,

"I'm killed!" John Lewis broke through the crowd first. But he was not the one who had yelled. Behind him, Austin Kotiza staggered out, clutching his throat form which blood was spurting from a knife slash.

Kotiza staggered into the saloon and up to the bar where he asked for a glass of water. While the barkeeper was getting the water, Kotiza staggered over to the far wall, still clutching the wound in his throat as if he could stem the flow of blood. There he stood until he suddenly slid to the floor, dead before he hit it, they said.

The man arrested for killing Kotiza was not Quinlan but Anton Moestrick. Moestrick was indicted for assault with intent to wound or kill. He was brought to trial in October, 1878, and found guilty.

Lowe Murder—Frontier County 1879

The winter of 1878 and 1879 was a very bad one. Cattle drifted for miles before the blizzard winds, looking for feed and shelter. Some drifted from Colorado over into Frontier County. At that time Frontier County extended from its current eastern boundary west to the Colorado border.

Cattle from the panhandle of Nebraska also drifted down into the county. All this necessitated a big roundup in the spring so the ranchers could sort out their cattle. Many cattle died in the bad weather and every rancher wanted to find as many of his own as he could. His chances of surviving the loss of so many cattle were slim at best.

Many men worked together on the roundup. The losses were apparent from the dead cattle piled up in gullies and against any obstacle that stopped their drifting. Tempers were short. When the gathered herds reached the mouth of Mitchell Creek, many of the horses the men were using were put in William Black's pasture overnight. Ike Lowe gathered up the horses the next morning and brought them into camp so the men could saddle up for the day's work. Joe Ansley's horse was not among those Lowe brought. The horse had apparently gotten out of the pasture during the night. Ansley had a short temper and he heaped blame on Lowe for not bringing in his horse. Lowe was short tempered, too, as were most of the men after the long, grueling, discouraging roundup.

Lowe and Ansley got into an argument

Furnas County's first courthouse
Nebraska, Our Towns

Isaac Burton's Trading Post, 1870s
Nebraska, Our Towns

after breakfast and the two went to a little pocket in the bluff and there they shot it out Ansley was faster with a gun and he killed Lowe. Then with his second shot he killed Lowe's horse.

When the men who had witnessed the fight rushed to take a hand, Ansley held his gun on them and stopped their approach while he caught a horse and rode away. Nobody was ready to ride so they couldn't follow him.

Lowe was buried there on the banks of Mitchell Creek. Sheriff McKnight was called in. He deputized two men, W.H. Miles and W.L. McClary, to go after Ansley and bring him back for trial.

After several days of hard riding which took the men up along the Platte River, they finally caught up with Ansley and brought him back to Frontier County.

Ansley hired E.T. Jay as his attorney. The trial was short; the evidence was clear because the incident itself was brief. The court found Ansley innocent of murder; it was ruled that Ansley shot in self defense. Ansley was turned free. Lowe's death was more a result of the hard drive to round up the surviving cattle than it was murder.

Rosier Murder—Furnas County   1878

Not all killings were done by guns or knives or even iron bars or hammers. In Furnas County shortly after the murder-suicide of Mrs. Colby and Willard Sawyer, a man named White and his wife tried a different method. They were living with a

Hauling manure from the barn to the field
Courtesy Nebraska State Historical Society

German bachelor named Rosier. Mrs. White was keeping house for the man and her husband was doing the work around the homestead. Rosier had plenty of money to pay them for their work. But they wanted more. They wanted not only all his money but his homestead, too.

The simplest method of doing away with Rosier without any fuss or remaining evidence was poison. So they put poison in the food that Mrs. White served him.

When he was dead, they took the body out behind the barn and buried it under a manure pile. They kept on working and living there as if Rosier were still alive, so it was some time before someone got curious and began searching and found the body in the manure pile.

The Whites were arrested and brought to trial. The evidence seemed to point to Mr. White as the instigator of the scheme. The man was sentenced to the penitentiary for life but the woman was acquitted.

Prairie Fire—Wayne County   1879

Nebraska has always been known for its prairie fires. With the breaking of the sod and farming, the fires became fewer and less destructive. But as long as there are large sections of grass, there will be prairie fires.

On October 18, 1879, a prairie fire erupted in Wayne County. There were many farms in the area but still there was a lot of unbroken prairie and once a spark touched that cured grass in the dry fall weather, a wild fire exploded, soon turning the country black.

This October fire swept across the prairie toward the W.E. Durin farm. Mrs. Durin was alone in the house at the time except for her very small daughter. The fire was threatening a shed that she particularly wanted to save. She decided to help the fire fighters. Grabbing a large piece of cloth, she soaked it in water and went out to do what she could to save the shed.

Mrs. Durin was a large woman and not particularly agile. She carried the baby with one arm rather than leave her unattended in the house. In running across a dry patch of grass between her house and the shed, she stumbled and fell.

Prairie fires pushed by a strong Nebraska wind move very fast. Before Mrs. Durin could get to her feet, the fire swept in and caught

Fighting a prairie fire
*Courtesy Nebraska State
Historical Society*

Wayne, 1886. Speed limit for horses, 6 mph.
Nebraska, Our Towns

Richardson Murder— Franklin County 1880

her clothing on fire. Not able to get up, she cradled the baby in her arms, trying to protect it from the fire. But by the time other fire fighters rushed to her rescue, she was terribly burned. Neither she nor her baby survived, victims of another of Nebraska's hazards facing the homesteaders on the plains.

Charles Wilkinson was employed as a hotel runner by Jacob Barnett, owner of the Tremont House in Bloomington. Wilkinson was a lover of the bottle and he often went on a week long drinking spree. That was the case in late February, 1880.

William Richardson was a friend of Wilkinson and they were together most of the afternoon of February 21. Wilkinson decided he wanted to go to a restaurant for oysters and invited Richardson to go along. Richardson accepted the invitation.

During the meal, Wilkinson got into a quarrel with the owner of the restaurant and finally stabbed him in the back. The wound was not fatal and the man escaped. Wilkinson decided he had to finish what he had started and he hurried back to the hotel to get his gun.

Once he had his gun, he started back

The old narrow Bloomington bridge
Nebraska, Our Towns

toward the restaurant. Richardson had not gone with Wilkinson but now he did start out, apparently hoping to stop Wilkinson before he did any more damage. He met Wilkinson in the middle of the street.

Wilkinson began calling Richardson names because he hadn't helped him in his argument with the restaurant owner. Wilkinson finally demanded that Richardson get down on his knees in the street and beg Wilkinson's pardon for being a coward. This Richardson refused to do. Wilkinson raised his gun and fired five times. Four of the bullets hit Richardson, killing him instantly.

Wilkinson then returned to the hotel to get more ammunition for his gun so he could go after the restaurant owner. In the hotel, he got his cartridges but was surrounded by the men of town who were determined to arrest him. However, Wilkinson waved his gun around and promised to shoot any man who laid a hand on him. It was a stand-off.

Jacob Barnet, owner of the hotel, grabbed a double-barreled shotgun and pointed it at Wilkinson and demanded he drop his gun or he'd blow him up. Wilkinson suddenly lost his bravery and, terrified, dropped his gun. The men swarmed over Wilkinson and took him off to jail. It was only after the excitement was over that Barnet discovered that the shotgun was not loaded.

Wilkinson was tried at the next term of the District Court. He was found guilty, but not of first degree murder. Using the lame excuse that he was drunk at the time, he was allowed to plead guilty to second degree murder. Judge Gaslin sentenced him to the penitentiary for life.

Elmer Parker Murder—
Johnson County   1880

Tecumseh prided itself in having no major crimes in its early days. But then politics raised its ugly head. There was a political

issue on the streets of town on June 25, 1880.

W.F. Parker, a bricklayer, got into a quarrel with Fred Blum. The argument got out of hand and the two men resorted to blows. The possibility of avoiding a fight was nullified by the fact that Parker's peaceful tendencies were blotted out by whiskey.

Parker's son, Elmer, got his father out of the fight and began leading him home. Blum, not satisfied with a draw in the argument, gathered several of his friends and went after Parker.

Elmer couldn't get his father home ahead of the pursuing men and they caught up with them. There were six men, led by Fred Blum and a young man eager to get into the fray, Henry Parrish. They launched an assault on the older Parker. Elmer was only seventeen but he tried to protect his father and get him away.

Henry Parrish picked up a large stone and slammed it against Elmer Parker's head. Parker dropped to the ground as if he'd been killed. That took the fight out of the others and they left hurriedly.

Elmer Parker was injured worse than anyone thought and he died from the blow. Henry Parrish and the other five men were all brought to trial for the murder. The prosecuting attorney called the attack totally unprovoked. Elmer Parker had simply been trying to get his father home.

Henry Parrish who had hit Elmer with the stone drew fifteen years in the penitentiary while the other five men each drew thirty days in jail and a hundred-dollar fine.

The case created a lot of excitement in Tecumseh and resulted in the closing of all the saloons in town for a year.

Bower Murder—Douglas County   1880

The dance was held at the home of H.D. Kirby in rural Douglas County. It wasn't

Two-horse streetcar in front of Jacob's Block, 1875
Courtesy Douglas County Historical Society

had each taken a girl to the dance. Bower's partner, although about the age of Pickard, was Pickard's aunt. There was bad blood between Pickard and Bower and apparently the fact that Bower was escorting Pickard's aunt to the dance stirred up that bad blood.

Pickard was playing the fiddle for the dance but he had had too much to drink, and quit part way through the evening and dropped down to sleep for a couple of hours. Lomany Bower took up the fiddle and played until Pickard revived. That evidently did not soothe Pickard's feelings.

Friends of Bower saw trouble coming and suggested to him that he should leave early to avoid it. Bower took the advice and he and his partner for the evening started for home. A cousin of Pickard's, named Burns, told Pickard that Bower was running out. Pickard dropped his fiddle and ran outside to catch Bower.

Earlier, as they were coming to the dance, Pickard had driven his buggy past Bower's buggy and demanded to know if Bower was there. No one answered and Pickard made the remark that he could lick Bower and added he could also put lead through him. It

exactly a Christmas dance but it had a sobering effect on Christmas.

The dance was held on December 14, 1880. Lomany Bower and Lorenzo Pickard

Wagons and sleds breaking a trail
through town
Nebraska, Our Towns

was Pickard's aunt who reproved him for what he'd said.

Bower's friend, M.E. Worley, left the dance with Bower. Also, Lomany Bower's brother went along. Pickard and his cousin ran after the rig that Bower was driving. It was too dark to see exactly what Pickard did, but they saw him stoop down and pick up something then throw it at Bower.

There was a dull thud and Lomany Bower fell out of the buggy onto the ground. Pickard rushed up and began beating on him. Burns pulled a gun and held off Bower's brother who was trying to go to Lomany's aid. Michael Worley finally pulled Pickard off Bower who was unconscious, the result of the blow to the head from the rock or hard object that Pickard had thrown.

Pickard left and the others carried Lomany Bower back to the house. Bower lingered between life and death for almost ten days. Then he died. The coroner's inquest was held Christmas morning and the jury ruled that Bower had died from a blow of a blunt instrument in the hands of or thrown by Lorenzo Pickard.

In the meantime, officers had found Pickard and arrested him. They were still looking for Burns to charge him with being an accessary. But they had the real killer. There was no doubt of Pickard's guilt.

Lupin Paxton Murder—
Howard County   1881

The jail in St. Paul in Howard County was the recipient of a murderer in June of 1881 and soon became the victim of an escape.

Lupin Paxton, twenty-one years old, was plowing in his father's field on June 8 when another young man, Hendry Tedrhan, eighteen, came out into the field to talk to him. There is no record of what was said, but young Paxton was an easy going fellow and Tedrhan was a not-too-bright unpredictable man, so it was assumed that there probably

was no argument. When Paxton turned away, Tedrhan pulled a pistol and shot Paxton in the head. Then, fearing he was not dead, Tedrhan grabbed the neckyoke off the nearby wagon and beat Paxton over the head, crushing his skull. As if this wasn't enough, he tied a rope around Paxton's neck and fastened the other end of the rope to the plow then drove the team part way across the field. There he unhitched the team and hitched them to the wagon and drove away.

When Lupin Paxton didn't come in from the field for supper, his younger brother, Charles, got on a horse and rode out to bring him in. He found Lupin dead, his body still tied to the plow.

The Paxtons were devastated. The neighbors joined them in going in search of the murderer, although they had no idea who it was. They found the wagon the next day and one horse. Continuing the search for the other horse, they finally found it not too far from the Tedrhan farm. They immediately suspected Henry Tedrhan.

Going to the Tedrhan farm, they found Henry planting corn. As soon as he saw the riders, he left his planter and began running. They went after him and even though they were on horseback, it took them three miles to catch the suspect.

He denied knowing anything about Lupin Paxton's murder, even after they found a bloody pair of overalls that belonged to him. Eventually, Henry broke down and confessed, relating all the details of the murder as unconcerned as if he were reading a story out of a book.

Henry Tedrhan was lodged in the jail at St. Paul but, a short time later, escaped from the jail. In disguise, he went to Grand Island, just to the south, and there he got a job with a farmer.

In the meantime, information had filtered in to explain the motive Henry Tedrhan might have had for killing Lupin Paxton. It

"Stone Block" building, where trials were held in early Hastings

Courtesy Adams County Historical Society

The mob seemed to know exactly where the prisoners were being held. They stormed up the stairs, yelling and making more noise than an army. They found the door to the room with the prisoners locked, so they employed the battering ram. It took two smashes with most of the men at the ram to crash through the door. Then they rushed in, thirty-three men, all masked and armed. The guards were quickly overwhelmed.

The prisoners were ordered down the stairs and into the street where a buggy was waiting. Inghram and Green were forced into the buggy while Babcock had to walk behind the buggy with a rope around his neck. All the guards were forced to come along, apparently to keep them from organizing a rescue party.

It was a little after ten o'clock when most of the town should have been asleep. But the noise created by the movements of the mob had brought many people out on the street. They followed the caravan as it moved to the north. None got too close to the masked men who ringed the buggy as it moved along.

Just a short distance to the north there was a bridge where the Grand Island and St. Joseph Railroad crossed High Street. That was where the buggy stopped. The two men inside were jerked out of the buggy and lined up with Babcock then marched up the railroad grade and out to the center of the bridge. All had ropes already around their necks. Some of the crowd followed. The loose ends of the ropes were fastened to the railroad ties or tracks.

True to his promise to John Babcock, Charles Dietrich spoke up in defense of the boy, explaining that he had helped them identify the killers and how he had been pulled into the scheme by the older men. The masked men would listen to none of that. All three were going to pay for their crime.

Dietrich tried to break through and take the rope off Babcock's neck but he was shoved back. Dietrich was a determined man; he'd made a promise and he intended to keep it.

Scene of the lynching of Fred Inghram and Jas. Green, murderers of C. M. Millett by the bold "33" on Tuesday night, April 3rd, 1883, at Hastings, Nebraska. Photographed by Geo. O. Churchill, Hastings, Nebr.

Scene the morning after Fred Inghram and James Green were lynched
Courtesy Adams County Historical Society

Potter's Field, where Inghram and Green were buried
Courtesy Adams County Historical Society

First Inghram was shoved off the bridge and the short rope jerked tight as he hit the end of it. Green followed in short order. Then it was Babcock's turn. Just as they shoved him off the bridge, Dietrich slashed the rope with his knife. Babcock fell to the ground under the bridge, unhurt.

Screams of rage came from some of the leaders of the mob. But there were some in the group who had suddenly had their fill of lynching when they looked at the dangling bodies of Inghram and Green. They shouted back that Dietrich had a right to say his piece. Dietrich explained that Babcock's confession had been the key to the solving of the crime. For that, he deserved another chance.

Dietrich was convincing and the growing crowd had seen all the lynching they wanted for one night. Resentment at flaunting the law was growing against the Committee of Thirty-Three so the leaders agreed to let Babcock wait for a legal trial.

A few weeks later, Babcock was tried and sentenced to ten years in the penitentiary, and there he learned the stone cutting trade. Someone speculated in later years that Babcock likely remembered, as he cut names in headstones, how close he had come to needing a stone for himself. But if he had died that night of April 4, 1883, he would likely have been buried with his two companions in the town's Potter's Field, with no stone to mark his grave.

The one benefit of the lynching was that it put a damper on the robberies and burglaries that had been plaguing Hastings. No one seemed to want to tempt the Committee of Thirty-Three again.

Sherwood Murder—
Gosper County   1884

Jonas Nelson was, according to the Cambridge Monitor of December 20, 1884,

"an old Swede of bad reputation." He had located a homestead along Medicine Creek in 1879. There was timber along the creek here, and Nelson's homestead included a good portion of fine timber.

In 1881, a young man, Eugene Sherwood, and his widowed mother settled on a homestead along the creek that joined Nelson's place. Sherwood's claim also had a good stand of timber on it.

Both Nelson and Sherwood sold wood to the neighbors who had claims back from the creek where there was no timber. This timber proved to be a sore point between Nelson and Sherwood.

Jonas Nelson apparently was a greedy man and he began cutting wood that Sherwood claimed was on his land. Nelson, in return, screamed that Sherwood was cutting timber off his land. Gene Sherwood had a survey made of the land and the boundary was clearly marked. But Nelson disagreed with the survey, claiming that it gave Sherwood far too much of the timber.

Jonas Nelson always carried two revolvers and looked like a man hunting for a war. When he went to town or around the neighborhood, he usually carried a double-barreled shotgun, too. With his disposition, people tended to avoid him when possible.

Gene Sherwood couldn't avoid him if he intended to keep a grip on the timber on his claim. And that timber was the main source of income for him and his mother. Each time Sherwood and Nelson met, they quarreled. Nelson threatened Sherwood but Sherwood held his ground. He was right, and the legal survey proved it. He pointed this out to Nelson, but Nelson was convinced that Sherwood, and every other neighbor who agreed with him, was determined to cheat him out of his timber. A legal survey meant nothing to him.

The situation came to a sudden head on Tuesday, December 16, 1884. Gene

Land where the deer and the antelope play
Nebraska, Our Towns

a look at his hand and accused Nelson of shooting himself. Then he left Nelson and ran to the trees to find Sherwood to see if he could help him.

In the timber, he found a couple of woodcutters who had located Sherwood's body. Gammil reported the crime to his neighbors and someone got word to the sheriff. Other neighbors gathered as soon as word got around. They began their own investigation, already convinced that Jonas Nelson had cold-bloodedly murdered Gene Sherwood. Some of the women had to take care of Mrs. Sherwood, Gene's mother. Her son had been her only means of support. Now she had not only lost her son, but also her means of survival.

Sherwood went out to hunt up some cows that had strayed away. He took his rifle, telling his mother he hoped to get a shot at a deer in the timber. It was cold and there was snow on the ground.

He didn't find his cattle; he didn't see a deer. He didn't even see Jonas Nelson moving through the trees toward him. Nelson sneaked along until he stood behind a big tree only a few feet from the path that Sherwood was following. Sherwood was within a few feet of that tree when Nelson stepped out with his shotgun cocked and leveled. It is doubtful if Sherwood even had time to realize his danger.

The shotgun roared and the top of Sherwood's head was blown completely off. As one report stated, his brains were spattered against a tree trunk.

A short time later Jonas Nelson appeared at the house of a neighbor, Jim Gammil. He didn't have his guns with him and one hand was dripping blood. Nelson showed Gammil the hand and said Sherwood had shot him and, in self defense, he had shot and killed Sherwood.

Gammil didn't believe Nelson. Like all his neighbors, he didn't trust him at all. He took

James M. Gammil, Jonas Nelson's neighbor. He reported Nelson's crime, and it was from his house that the mob dragged Nelson.
Courtesy Frontier County Museum

The neighbors didn't wait for the sheriff to arrive. They began looking for evidence that would confirm what they all believed. They went to Nelson's place. There they found

William and Margaret Allen, parents of Theresa Gammil
Courtesy Frontier County Museum

The coroner's jury stated that Jonas Nelson had come to his death by hanging by party or parties unknown. And there the matter rested. No one tried to find the parties responsible.

Taylor Lynching—Clay County 1885

When Judge Lynch held court, the trial was usually short, the sentence brief, the execution swift, and there was no appealing the verdict.

Down on the western edge of Clay County, southeast of Hastings, trouble began brewing in 1880 and took five years to reach its climax. James and Elizabeth Taylor had

where Nelson had gone to show his wounded hand and tell about the battle he'd had with Sherwood. Gammil hadn't believed Nelson then. And it was Gammil who had filed the complaint with Judge Allen to have Nelson arrested for murder. That hardly seemed the place for Nelson to be taken for safe keeping. Also this was very close to the scene of the tragedy—another reason why this was a poor location to take Nelson.

Maybe the mob was forming before the preliminary hearing was over. Maybe the sheriff was totally in favor of the mob's plans. At any rate, sometime during the night, the mob struck at Gammil's and kidnapped Nelson. There are no details of the capture of Nelson by the mob. There are no details of what the mob did after they got Nelson. However, the final result was obvious to all the next morning.

Jonas Nelson's body was found hanging from a limb of the very tree where he had hidden before he stepped out and shot Gene Sherwood. The Regulators had cut Nelson's throat, shot him, and hung him out to freeze.

Vigilante justice was swift and very sure. In rare instances it went astray and strung up the wrong man, but, in this case, there was no doubt in anyone's mind. There had been no mistake.

The advertisement that brought thousands to the Nebraska plains, expecting to get rich in a hurry
Courtesy Jane Graff

A homestead near a creek where logs were available

Courtesy Nebraska State Historical Society

settled on some land on the Little Blue River in the spring of 1872, just three years after they were married. They were of Welsh descent, and other Welshmen as well as Bohemians settled around them.

By 1880 the country was filling up fast. The Taylors loaned money to many newcomers to help them get started. James Taylor had three quarters of land, and in 1881, he broke out 85 acres of it for farming. Immediately there was trouble caused by neighbors' cattle breaking into Taylor's field, and Taylor's cattle breaking down fences to get into other farmers' fields.

It soon seemed that the Taylor cattle and horses were getting into fields of the neighbors with infuriating regularity. After

learning of the verdict in the trial of "Print" Olive in Hastings, the farmers not only made it clear that Taylor's cattle had to be kept securely fenced away from their fields but they demanded payment for damages when they got out. Elizabeth Taylor resented those demands. They had worked hard to get a little herd of cattle and she didn't propose to pay greedy neighbors for something she was sure was not their fault. She began accusing the neighbors of deliberately tearing down the Taylor fences so the cattle would get into the fields and the neighbors could demand payment for the damages.

James Taylor was a mild mannered man and he paid the damages whenever it was proved that their cattle had been in the other man's fields. Elizabeth was not that easy going. She wasn't bashful in letting everybody know what she suspected. When it became obvious that James Taylor was not going to argue the point, Elizabeth proceeded to work on her husband to get him to deed everything over to her so she could handle the business that he disliked so much. He finally agreed. The minute she got the deeds in her name, she demanded that the neighbors they had loaned money to pay up. Ironically, those were the same neighbors who had been demanding payment for damages done to their crops. With the law on her side, Elizabeth collected from all her neighbors who owed the Taylors money. It didn't set well with those neighbors.

Suddenly, in May of 1882, James Taylor died. The coroner's report said he died of natural causes but neighbors, already smarting with resentment at the high-handed way Elizabeth was running her place, were ready to jump on any hint of treachery on her part. That hint came from a Bohemian neighbor who had happened to be fishing in the Little Blue River when James Taylor galloped his horse down to the river and jumped off, running to the river bank and gulping down water. By the time the settler had dropped his fishing pole and gone over to Taylor, he had fallen face down in the water and the settler found him already dead.

Then some neighbor lady recalled that she had seen Elizabeth Taylor buying a fair amount of potato bug killer a few months before. The potent ingredient in the bug killer was paris green. There were those who jumped to the conclusion that Elizabeth, disgusted at her weak-kneed husband, had helped him end his miserable subservient existence. Even though there was no proof of such treachery, Elizabeth's eager neighbors reveled in the possibility that it was true, and watched for further evidence that she was a menace to every citizen of the community.

Elizabeth's father died that fall and was buried in the local cemetery. Then Elizabeth reversed her position in wanting to control everything on her place and turned over the business dealings of the little ranch to her brother, Tom Jones.

One of Elizabeth's admirers was Rees T. Rees, another Welshman. But he didn't meet with her approval and she bluntly sent him packing. His pride was hurt and his resentment toward her grew until he became her worst enemy. It was thought that he might have started the rumor concerning the disappearance of the Taylor hired hand, Ben Bethlemer. It was suggested that he might have gotten a dose of that potato bug killer. Elizabeth didn't even bother to respond to the rumor.

Tom Jones and his sister decided to go back into cattle ranching only and stop farming. That meant more cattle and more fences. But their resources didn't stretch far enough to hire the men they needed to take care of the livestock. Elizabeth came up with the idea of posting a notice in town that anybody willing to work for board and room would be welcome at their place. The offer was accepted by several different men. Most of them came and worked for a while then moved on. Neighbors, watching Elizabeth Taylor closely now, quickly seized on the constant coming and going of strangers as proof that this was a cattle rustling gang, headed by the Taylor woman. Since there was no evidence to support the claim, nothing was done about it; but the rumors persisted and grew.

For safety's sake, Elizabeth bought a shotgun, the only one in the neighborhood, so far as was known. Now she felt secure from anyone who might try to harm her or any of her family.

In the spring of 1884, a man named Edwin Roberts brought his family to the Little Blue from Wales. He settled on land

The most common means of transportation in Elizabeth Taylor's day
Courtesy Jane Graff

adjoining the Taylor-Jones land. For a time they were friendly neighbors, then the rumors reached Mrs. Roberts and she accepted what she heard as truth and the friendship was cut off.

More fences were torn down and more demands for damage lodged against Elizabeth Taylor and her brother, Tom Jones. But the real burr under the saddle came when neighbors, especially the newcomer, Edwin Roberts, began cutting trees and hauling lumber from the tree claim that Elizabeth had taken some years before.

Elizabeth filed a complaint but nothing could be done until the case was settled in court. In the meantime, Roberts and another neighbor were cutting trees and hauling them away as fast as they could. On January 8, 1885, Elizabeth saw Roberts and his neighbor heading for the tree claim and she knew they were going to cut another load of trees. She screamed at them but they ignored her.

Elizabeth's two sons, about twelve and eleven now, had been absorbing the anger of the feud and they apparently took a hand in things. Their mother had hired a young man from Texas to ride the fences to keep them from being torn down. This hired man and the two boys got into a wagon and headed for the tree claim.

They met Roberts and his neighbor, Joseph Beyer, coming from the tree claim with their wagon piled high with logs. The boys screamed curses at the men and the noise frightened the team. Beyer, riding on the logs, fell off into the road. The team raced on with Roberts driving. Beyer swore he heard a shot. When other neighbors stopped the team farther down the road, they discovered Edwin Roberts dead in the wagon, half his head blown away. One of the Rees boys reported that he had seen the Taylor wagon race by their place with William, Elizabeth's older son, holding a shotgun.

So the Taylor boys were arrested and thrown in jail, charged with murder, although there were no actual witnesses to the killing. Their case was scheduled to be

Wagons were used to haul sod, logs, and even boys with guns.
Courtesy Jane Graff

heard in May. That was too long a wait for the neighbors of Elizabeth and Tom Jones. They were not concerned about the boys. They were determined to get rid of Elizabeth Taylor and her brother.

Rees T. Rees reportedly started the talk of running the unwanted woman and her brother out of the country. Others quickly fell in with him. In early March, these men called together fifty to seventy-five men who rode to Elizabeth's fairly new frame house and demanded that she and her brother come out. Their reply was a volley of shots that convinced most of the raiders to go home. Many were Bohemian and didn't speak English. All they knew about what they were doing was what others had told them in their language. What they'd heard didn't include a gun battle. With their small army gone, the ring leaders backed off, too. Elizabeth and her brother had won the first round of the war.

The next day they moved from Elizabeth's frame house down to the sod house they had originally lived in. Those thick walls were bullet proof; the frame house wasn't.

A bullet-proof sod house
Courtesy Nebraska State Historical Society

A night or two later, the barn of John Llewelyn, one of the ring leaders who had crossed words many times with Elizabeth, was burned. Of course, she was blamed. It rekindled the fire that had been partly snuffed out a few nights before by the bullets coming from Elizabeth's frame house.

One report did not mention the first attempt to run Elizabeth and her brother out of the country. But none of the reports skipped the meeting on March 14. The preliminary action to this meeting almost guaranteed the success of the venture this time.

Elizabeth had gone to Hastings that day and her mother, her brother Tom, and her little daughter had also gone away, likely to visit the two boys who were in jail awaiting their trial for the murder of Edwin Roberts. Someone had conveniently slipped into Elizabeth's sod house and stolen all the guns and ammunition she had stored there. There would be no gun battle when the supporters of Judge Lynch came calling this night.

Many of the Bohemians who had been sucked into the first raid knew what was in store this time and did not show up. But there were still about fifty men who were convinced that the country had to get rid of Elizabeth Taylor and her brother, Tom Jones.

Shortly after midnight, the men who had gathered across the bridge from the Taylor soddy walked over the iron and wooden bridge and shuffled up to the door. Some moved around to guard the windows so that no one inside could escape. One of the ring leaders yelled for the people inside to come out. It took the third yell to bring them out. With no guns or ammunition inside, the occupants had little choice.

The five men who came out first were searched and their hands tied behind their backs, and five men were designated to guard them. The last two out were Elizabeth and her brother, Tom. They were grabbed and their hands jerked behind them and tied. Elizabeth screamed for a chance to get some warm clothes on. She was wearing only her nightgown. But all she got was a shawl that someone found just inside the soddy door.

Judge Lynch presided then at the brief trial. Accusations flew at the two, mainly Elizabeth. Her only concession was that she

had persuaded her brother to hire someone to burn John Llewelyn's barn. That seemed to be enough to convince the mob of her guilt on all counts.

They sent the first five men who had come out of the soddy away with a guard, to be released with instructions never to show their faces in the country again. They turned Elizabeth and Tom toward the bridge, less than a hundred yards away, and told them to march.

Elizabeth surely expected nothing worse than a tongue lashing and an order to get out of the country and never come back. Nobody did worse than that to a woman. It was only when they reached the bridge and she saw the men tying ropes to the bridge that she realized what her fate and that of her brother was to be.

They both pleaded for their lives, insisting that they had not murdered anyone or done anything worthy of hanging. But the lynchers were determined that nothing was going to stop them from getting rid of their irritating neighbors.

All reports agree on what happened next but disagree on how it happened. One report said the ropes were fastened to the bridge and the two victims were pushed off the bridge just as had been done to the killers of Cassius Millet on the bridge in north Hastings. Others said that the two were marched down under the bridge and into the cold water to a sand bar in the middle of the creek and there they were put on horses. A gun was fired, startling the horses into a wild gallop, leaving the two victims swinging from their ropes.

In either case, it marked the end of the career of the only woman to be lynched in Nebraska. The only crime that they had proof she had committed was the ordering of the burning of John Llewelyn's barn.

Broadway Street in Scottsbluff,
1900
*Courtesy Nebraska State
Historical Society*

several years did the state legislature appro-
priate seven thousand dollars to Scottsbluff
County to help pay for the costs of the trial.
Nellie M. Richardson, the former wife of the
prosecuting attorney at the trial, claimed that
she was responsible for the passage of the bill
for she had lobbied for it. She filed for pay
for her efforts as a lobbyist. When that was
denied, she filed suit for $1500. That, too,
was denied.

George Arnold had spent some time in the
prison when he was judged to be insane, and
he was transferred to the insane asylum just
west of Hastings. After being there a while,
they declared him cured and he was released.
He lost no time in getting out of Nebraska.

Edward Maher Murder—
Chase County   1889

On March 27, 1889, Edward Maher went
into Imperial, the county seat of Chase
County, which was only three years old.
There he borrowed two hundred dollars on
his homestead, because there was nothing to
live on until the crop he intended to plant
came in. Although it was quite a distance to

town, he walked in, got the loan, and walked
back to the northeast toward his homestead.

Maher passed close to the homestead of
Miles Henry. Exactly what took place
between the two is not known, but
apparently the fact that Maher had two
hundred dollars in his pocket became known
to Henry. That was the equivalent of a
fortune in those money-scarce days.

Henry, mounted on his horse, made a
quick decision to take that money. That
would be much faster and easier than
working an entire summer and hoping the
weather cooperated so he could earn that
much. Bringing his gun to bear on the
homesteader, he ordered him to march over
the hill. Maher probably suspected he was
going to be robbed but he likely didn't expect
what Henry had in mind.

Once over the hill, Henry deliberately shot
Maher in the back of the head then took his
money. Realizing that, even though he had
eliminated all eye witnesses to his crime,
there would be a thorough investigation of
the dead man and how he met his death,
Henry headed north on his horse, sure that

Interior of store in early Imperial

Courtesy Chase County Historical Museum

he could disappear before the law could catch up with him.

When it became known that Edward Maher hadn't reached home the day he had gone to Imperial, a search for him began. Sheriff G.W. Rogers suspected foul play when he was told that Maher had borrowed two hundred dollars from the bank that day.

The search located Maher's body with the bullet hole in the back of the head. Henry had overlooked one thing in his effort to escape the finger of suspicion. Henry's horse had lost a shoe on one front foot, and neighbors knew about that. That horse with only one shoe had left tracks that identified it. Most people who shod their horses put shoes only on the front feet, but they made sure they were on both front feet.

The sheriff looked for Miles Henry and discovered that he had left the country. That confirmed the sheriff's conviction that Henry was the murderer. It wasn't long after that when Sheriff Rogers heard that Henry was working on a ranch in northern Nebraska. He went there and was told at the ranch that Henry was working with the crew. With the foreman's help, he waited until the crew came in, then Rogers stepped up behind the unsuspecting Henry with a drawn gun. Henry had no chance to escape.

The sheriff brought Henry back to Chase County, and first degree murder charges

Early street scene in Imperial
*Courtesy Chase County
Historical Museum*

West side of Main Street, Imperial
Nebraska, Our Towns

were filed against him. It would be the first murder trial in Chase County when district court convened on June 27, 1889.

The evidence was conclusive, but the jury brought in a verdict of guilty of second degree murder. Few understood that since it had been a deliberate murder, it was a first degree offense. On the decision of the jury, the judge handed down a sentence on July 1, of confinement in the state penitentiary at hard labor and on March 27 of each year he was in prison, he should be kept in solitary confinement.

His wife sued for divorce, which was granted, and she took their three-year-old daughter and also took back her maiden name. The loss of both his wife and daughter added to the punishment Miles Henry had received.

Mob County—Keyapaha County 1889

Keyapaha County earned its nickname of Mob County in the 1880s and 1890s. The Niobrara River formed the southern boundary of the county. There were many deep canyons running down from the northern prairie to the Niobrara River, and these formed avenues of escape for the fugitives from the law south of the Niobrara. Keyapaha County had more than its share of law breakers within its boundary, most of them from other areas.

Doc Middleton, among others, used the canyons on the north side of the Niobrara at times for his hideout. The law in Keyapaha County was unable to cope with the influx of horse and cattle thieves. There were citizens in the county who felt they could do the job themselves if they were given the chance. So Vigilance Committees came into being.

A typical homestead in north central Nebraska
Courtesy Nebraska State Historical Society

People who owned a good horse or a good team lived in dread that they would be stolen. No matter how closely the owners watched their animals, they seemed to disappear as if by magic. The only solution, the way the settlers saw it, was to stop the trouble at the source. They went after the thieves themselves.

They gathered any bit of information they could find that pointed a suspicious finger at anyone who might be doing the stealing. Most of their information was reliable but some, no doubt, was not. Some people, who did little more than lend a helping hand to

someone who seemed to need it, found themselves trying to explain to the vigilantes that they were totally innocent of any implication in the theft of any horses or cattle.

In a span of a couple of years from 1889 to 1891, Keyapaha County made a name for itself. But it also earned the reputation of not being a hospitable place for horse thieves. Even neighbors began to look sharply at other neighbors, and tried to walk such a straight narrow path that the vigilantes could not suspect them of sticky fingers that clung to the ropes of strange horses.

Maupin Murder—Keyapaha County

The vigilantes in Keyapaha County began to hit full stride in 1889. The horse thieves of the past few years were now, in February, 1889, taking cattle. That was hitting the ranchers even harder than losing a few horses now and then. Small herds of cattle were being driven off and sold to buyers who were not too particular about the brands on the cattle.

The vigilantes were convinced that George Babcock was one of the leaders of these thieves and set out to let all the thieves in the county see what happened to their kind. They heard that Babcock was in the county seat, Springview, and went there to find him.

Surmising that he was probably staying in the Tremont Hotel, they went there about midnight and asked the clerk on duty, Fred Burnham, if Babcock and another man on their list, C. M. Clay, were in. Burnham told them that neither was in right then. He was sure that was the truth, but it was learned later that both were in the hotel and well armed.

Earlier that day, Sheriff Coble had arrested a man that some suspected of being a rustler. He was posing as a cattle buyer, but he was not particular about whose cattle he

View on South Main Street,
Springview
*Courtesy Keyapaha County
Historical Society*

Keyapaha County Courthouse,
Springview
Nebraska, Our Towns

bought. Some of the vigilantes felt that a buyer should be sure he was buying cattle from the real owner and not taking cattle that had been stolen. They felt that Arthur Maupin was anything but careful about ownership, and might even be helping the rustlers in rounding up the cattle for sale.

Sheriff Coble had suggested that he take his business some place other than Keyapaha County. Maupin ignored the request and was downright belligerent. He was well armed.

It was while Arthur Maupin was eating dinner at the Tremont Hotel that the sheriff moved up behind him with drawn gun and arrested him. Maupin had no chance to fight back. There were too many unanswered questions about Maupin's activities that needed clearing up. Maupin was anything but cooperative, so Sheriff Coble took him to the courthouse and put him in the steel cage in the wooden jail just behind the courthouse. He was hoping that a night in the jail would loosen his tongue.

The sheriff wasn't even sure where Maupin came from. Some said O'Neill, Nebraska, and some said Fort Pierre, South Dakota. Maupin wouldn't admit to either. That only increased the suspicions of the sheriff. No telling where he would take the cattle he was supposedly buying here in Keyapaha County.

But the sheriff was only thinking of his own method of getting Maupin to talk. He hadn't taken into account the vigilantes and their methods of dealing with suspicious characters. With the vigilantes, it was reaching the point where suspicion was tantamount to conviction of guilt.

Sometime during the latter part of the night, the vigilantes struck. They had failed to find George Babcock in town but they knew where Maupin was. They broke into the wooden jail and riddled Maupin with bullets in his steel cage. The coroner could only report that Maupin had come to his death at the hands of persons unknown.

Newell Murder—Keyapaha County   1889

John T. Newell, thirty-four and unmarried, lived about twenty miles northeast of Springview near the Keyapaha River. Nobody could accuse him of stealing either horses or cattle. But he was a generous man who would willingly share anything he had with anyone who needed it. It was a habit that the vigilantes considered a fault.

On several occasions he put up passersby who asked for a night's lodging, and on a few such nights, his visitors were the men the vigilantes were trying to capture. It was known that the vigilantes considered Newell on the wrong side of the law when he allowed the horse thieves to spend the night with him.

Still, no one expected anything drastic to happen to the generous Newell. But on May 29, 1889, friends came to his house and found him dead. They had heard that the vigilantes had been riding the night before, but hadn't expected them to come after Newell.

Some reports say Newell was killed in bed; others say he was stretched out on the floor in his night clothes. There were twenty-four bullets in his body, and there was also some buck-shot. His own shotgun was lying between his legs with one barrel discharged. But it was impossible to suspect that this was a case of suicide. The door of his house was battered down and every window broken.

His crime had been harboring horse thieves.

Babcock Caught by Vigilantes in Keyapaha County   1889

George Babcock had been the prime target of the vigilantes since early in the year. They had been after him in February when they caught the man they thought had bought the stolen cattle, A.J. Maupin, and that arrest ended in Maupin's death. But Babcock was still at large.

Evidently, the vigilantes had expected to catch Babcock at Newell's place. Rumor had it that Newell had given shelter to Babcock. So John Newell paid with his life for that. But still Babcock was free.

Not finding Babcock at Newell's, the vigilantes went to the next home that was on their list of possible hiding places for George Babcock. That place was the home of his brother-in-law, T.V. Smith. It was only a few miles from Newell's place.

They arrived at Smith's place about three in the morning of May 30 and surrounded the house. Here they decided on a different tactic. If Babcock was there, it could be dangerous to get that close to the door. They had several rolls of cloth that they had soaked in kerosene. Striking a match, they set the rolls on fire. Quickly they threw those fire balls through the windows of Smith's house, setting the interior of the house on fire.

Then they waited, but not for long. The fire was exploding into an inferno. Everyone inside rushed into the yard in his night clothes. There was no time for making elaborate preparations to greet the visitors outside. George Babcock was one of the men who rushed out of the burning building. The vigilantes swarmed over him.

As soon as they had him tied up, they put him on a horse and started for the river. The destination was obvious. There were trees along the river with limbs big enough to hold up a swinging man.

It seems apparent what happened, but there were a variety of reports on what actually did take place. Here are three of the reports. The first is most likely—that Babcock was hanged from a tree limb. Another was that the vigilantes decided against hanging, but kept him in custody. Not likely. A third story said that he jabbed spurs to his horse and escaped. Where did he get his spurs? Did he sleep with them on? Take your choice of those three reports.

Lewis Murder—Hamilton County 1890

The sweep of homesteaders had about filled the western counties of Nebraska when an unexpected double tragedy hit the little town on Bromfield in Hamilton County, east of Grand Island.

Amos Staton lived about a mile south of Bromfield that March of 1890, just five years before the town's name was changed to Giltner. Staton was a bachelor, and his sister came to visit him that spring. Three men had ridden past the Staton farm and seen Amos's sister and, as young men are often prone to do, made some remarks in town about this lady.

Amos was very jealous of his sister, and he heard about these remarks and took serious exception to them. He learned that the three men were Al Dawson, William Lewis, and a young man named Berry.

Some people felt that Amos Staton was not the most stable man mentally in the area,

and perhaps his actions bore that out. He brooded over what he considered insults or degrading remarks about his sister and he set out that Saturday afternoon, March 15, to rectify things.

Taking his gun with him, he started out in search of the three men. He heard that Al Dawson was helping some friends haul hay and he headed that way. Seeing a load of hay coming, he motioned it down to inquire if Dawson was with them. One man quickly said that he had been but he had gone home. As soon as Staton had gone on, Al Dawson crawled out from under the hay. They had heard how furious Amos Staton was over what had been said and Dawson decided that hiding was better than possibly being shot at.

Staton walked on into Bromfield. On that particular day, Charles Harrod, who owned the meat market in town, had hired William Lewis to watch the store while he got some work done in his pelt room behind the market. Lewis, totally unaware that danger was threatening, was sitting next to the front window of the meat market reading a newspaper.

Staton saw him there and went around to come into the market through the back door. He passed by Charles Harrod working in the pelt room but each ignored the other. Staton had only one thing in mind, Lewis sitting at the front window reading. Harrod didn't notice anything unusual about Staton coming into the store and went on about his work.

Staton stepped into the meat market and spoke sharply to Lewis. "You're the man I've been looking for."

Before Lewis could get out of his chair, Staton pulled out his revolver and shot him in the chest. That shot and Lewis's scream echoed into the street and startled every person within hearing distance.

Lewis leaped out of his chair and raced toward the back door, maybe hoping that Harrod would help. But Staton was only a

A nice house in modern Giltner

Photo by author

step behind Lewis as the young man went out the back door, Staton shot him again in the back. Lewis fell, dying within minutes.

Staton turned back to the street, heading for the grain elevator where he'd heard that Berry was working this afternoon. It was about three o'clock on a Saturday afternoon, the busiest hour of the week for the town. One citizen, John Gallentine, overcame his shock and took a hand, stopping Staton from killing anyone else or escaping from town. He demanded that Staton halt, and he did. He handed Staton over to Marshal Frye, who promptly directed Staton toward the little jail that the town boasted where they held prisoners until the sheriff from Aurora could come and take them to a real jail in the county seat.

Marshal Frye disarmed Staton and locked him up, apparently without any opposition from Staton. The marshal then sent word to the sheriff at Aurora to come and get the murderer as quickly as possible.

Meanwhile, the people of town were

overcoming their surprise and shock, and talk buzzed along the street about what should be done. Some recommended caution, but others demanded immediate reprisal. Hanging was too good for a man who would kill an upstanding young man like William Lewis. His death left a widow and five children, but he was very well off financially so the family would not suffer from lack of money.

There was some difference of opinion, but the shock of the murder was driving normally stable men into violent reaction. A dozen men began gathering in front of Chapman's Implement Store and soon they disappeared inside. Everyone was anticipating the arrival of the sheriff from Aurora on the four o'clock train to take the prisoner back to the county seat.

Obviously that thought was also uppermost in the minds of the men in the implement shop. They didn't want to see Staton go to jail, and then somehow, at the trial, get himself off the hook. They wanted immediate punishment.

In a few minutes those men came out of the implement shop with masks over their faces and wearing their coats turned wrong side out. Even those who knew everybody in town and the surrounding country couldn't identify any of the men, although many must have known who had disappeared into that implement shop before these masked men came out.

One man had a rope, and as they marched up the street, some man down at the end of the street yelled, "There he goes into the field." Attention was suddenly diverted from the men going resolutely up the street toward the jail. Those who weren't distracted from the marching men saw that the rope one man was carrying had a noose in it.

At the jail, the men broke open the lock into the cell and dragged Staton out. It was about four o'clock now, almost time for the

Abandoned church in Giltner

Photo by author

train to arrive from Aurora. If the sheriff got here on time, the lynching would be stopped. The men hurried.

They almost ran Staton down to the livery barn where they threw the end of the rope over a cross beam, pulled the noose snugly around Staton's neck, and pulled him off the ground. Tying the end of the rope to a partition studding, they hurried back to the implement shop.

The train was late. By the time it arrived and Deputy Sheriff Whitesides, County Attorney Whitmore, City Marshal George Barschlin, and Coroner Elarton disembarked, there was no sign of the men who had come from the implement shop to lynch Staton. Likely they were now circulating among the many people who were still agog over the happenings of the afternoon.

The deputy sheriff moved importantly into the crowd, demanding to know if the prisoner was in the jail. Someone said he had been taken there. But when the officer found the jail empty, he demanded an explanation. Finally one man said the deputy might find

him in the livery barn. The men from Aurora looked, and they did find him, but not in time to save his life.

The coroner took over then. The first body to examine was that of Lewis. He impaneled a jury and called the witnesses who had seen the killing. He found plenty of them, and it didn't take long for the verdict to be reached. Lewis had died from gunshots fired by Amos Staton.

It took much longer for the coroner to complete the investigation into Staton's death. There was no doubt about what had happened, but the coroner found absolutely no one who could even give a hint as to who had helped lynch the murderer.

The only thing that the inquests really achieved was the knowledge that William Lewis was thirty-three years old, and that Amos Staton was forty-five years old and a bachelor. The little evidence that did come out suggested that Amos Staton might have been a little bit deranged mentally. If so, the lynching might not have been quite as justifiable as it had seemed at first.

But the coroner's jury could only reach the conclusion that Amos Staton had met his demise at the hands of parties unknown. As time went on and people had time to consider the situation, the lynching became less justifiable. There had been a murder and the murderer should have been punished. But Nebraska had laws for that. Those laws hadn't been given time to work. Still not a finger pointed to any man who had impeded the legal process.

Whether it was right or wrong might be debatable, but one thing was certain. Pioneer justice was usually swift and always irreversible.

Dayton-Rivers Murders— Keyapaha County   1891

A combination of events led to a shoot-out between neighbors along the Niobrara River, just downstream a ways from the little town of Carns. It all began with an underhanded trick two men played to get a high price for the land they wanted to sell.

They sprinkled some gold filings near a cliff on the land, then invited a wealthy lady and her new husband to come up from Stuart in western Holt County—a short distance south of the Niobrara River—for a picnic.

The lady had been a widow until recently. She was quite wealthy for those days and had become infatuated with a man more than thirty years younger than herself, Schuyler Dayton, and married him. They accepted the invitation to the picnic. While there, Mrs. Dayton discovered the gold filings scattered near the bluff and thought the gold had washed out of the bluff. She bought the land for a good price and the two men left the country, much richer for their deception.

Mrs. Dayton and her young husband moved onto the land and bought a good herd of cattle. They also brought some hired help, a man named John Rivers and his wife. Mrs. Dayton apparently discovered that the gold flakes had been a plant, but she still expected to make a good ranch out of the river land.

Downstream a short distance was George Covell. He was also a rancher and carried the mail from Carns to Springview, the county seat, to the northwest of Carns.

After some neighborhood squabbles during which John Rivers left his wife in a fit of anger but later repented and returned, real trouble suddenly erupted when George Covell accused Dayton and Rivers of stealing some of his cattle.

Schuyler Dayton and John Rivers were furious over the accusations and decided they would go to Covell's ranch and settle the affair, either through discussion, fists, or guns.

It was on May 22, 1891, when they drove Dayton's wagon down the river valley to the

Springview Flouring Mill, 1907
Courtesy Keyapaha County Historical Society

Covell ranch. They had with them a prize fighter from Norfolk named Richard Wooliscroft. They saw George Barto (Charlie Burt in some reports) going toward Covell's. Barto worked for Covell, so he was a prime target, too. Rivers and Wooliscroft went after him while Dayton drove on down the river bank till he came even with the Covell ranch. There he stopped and got out of the wagon to tie his team to a fence post.

Rivers and Wooliscroft caught Barto and started leading him back toward the wagon. Meantime, George Covell appeared on the bluff above the wagon with a shotgun.

Covell shot Dayton in the back, killing him almost instantly. Then he began running toward Rivers and Wooliscroft and their prisoner. Barto started yelling for Covell not to shoot. He might hit him. Covell did shoot, however, hitting Rivers in the hips, flattening him. Rivers got off one shot hitting Barto in the head.

Wooliscroft dropped his hold on Barto,

raced for the wagon, and made his escape while Covell was reloading his shotgun. The shoot-out that Dayton and Rivers had planned turned out to be a very one-sided affair.

Covell and Barto went to Springview and reported what had happened, making it look as much like self defense as possible.

Mrs. Rivers called a doctor from Stuart to tend to her husband. Neighbors actually came near the ranch and fired shots at it. They yelled that they wanted the Dayton and Rivers people out of their neighborhood. Some thought that Covell was behind these demonstrations.

John Rivers was told to stay quiet in bed but he was a poor patient. He tried often to sit up and, two days after the shooting, did manage to sit up for a moment. Then he dropped back and died a few minutes later. During the funeral for the two men, Dayton and Rivers, someone stole Dayton's fine team. Perhaps that was just another hint that the neighborhood wanted the Daytons and Rivers gone.

George Covell was tried in the district court of Keyapaha County and the jury returned a verdict of not guilty, ruling it self defense. Mrs. Dayton and Mrs. Rivers moved east to the newly established county of Boyd.

George Covell was a small man, cross-eyed, and some said he had a "touchy" temper. Less than three years after he killed Dayton and Rivers, he committed suicide by cutting his throat with a kitchen knife. The date was April 19, 1894. That seemed to be the final act in the battle between George Covell, Schuyler Dayton, and John Rivers. Nobody won.

Stevens Murder—Dawson County 1893

In the extreme southwest corner of Dawson County in the town of Farnam, trouble erupted on July 11, 1893. There had been a sharp difference of opinion between S.B. Walker, a rancher in the vicinity, and George Stevens, a homesteader.

Walker felt that there were too many settlers coming, plowing up the grass that the cattle needed. So far as he was concerned, this land was the way God meant it to be and the homesteaders had no right to try to improve on what God had done.

Walker had been giving his closest neighbors some trouble, and the homesteaders had appointed Stevens to try to reason with him. Stevens had met with Walker but the meeting had only heightened the trouble. Walker apparently brooded over the fact that he could not get rid of the farmers who were plowing up his grass.

On Tuesday, July 11, George Stevens was in the Dunham Drug Store on the west side of Main Street and left it to go directly across the street to the Buss & Dovoll Store. That was the moment when Walker's frustration snapped his judgment. He began shooting at Stevens at a range where he couldn't miss.

Stevens managed to get to the store he was aiming for, and there he collapsed. He had three bullet wounds. He died a few minutes later.

Walker was arrested quickly. There seemed to be no immediate cause for his actions. The district court session in Lexington was set for November 28, but the judge didn't arrive until late in the evening—so the court didn't begin until Wednesday, November 29. There were several minor cases that came up, so it was another couple of days later before they got the jury seated for the Walker trial. There had been a lot of publicity about the case back in the summer when the murder took place, and many people had read about it and had already made up their minds about the guilt or innocence of S.B. Walker.

The trial began the afternoon of December 1, with the state presenting its case with

Farnam, from south of the tracks,
overlooking stockyards
Nebraska, Our Towns

The Woods Hotel, at Farnam,
1888–1906
Courtesy Max McNickle

witnesses to back up their charge of first degree murder. On Saturday morning, the defense presented its case. The defense plea was insanity. Among the witnesses were several insanity experts.

Speculation in Farnam ran wild. After all, this was the first murder that had ever occurred in Farnam. It would be the last in all the town's early days. Many thought Walker would be convicted, but few thought he'd get a severe sentence.

The speculators were right in that he would be convicted, but wrong in their guess that he would get a light sentence. The jury obviously did not believe his plea of insanity. S. B. Walker was convicted of first degree

murder and the judge sentenced him to hang. That sentence was set to be carried out, but the governor stayed the execution at the last minute and commuted the sentence to life imprisonment.

In those days, life imprisonment sentences were not reduced to a few years. Walker died in prison several years later.

Jansen Murder—Frontier County   1897

1897 was a quiet time in southern Frontier County. Crime was not a big problem. An occasional theft of a horse was the biggest crime that could be expected.

But a quiet man, some would say an

Shaw Brothers' business,
Cambridge, 1900
Nebraska, Our Towns

Stockville, about at its zenith,
1900
Nebraska, Our Towns

eccentric man, disappeared and only a few noticed. Thomas Jansen was a widower and a loner. He was called the Indianola Millionaire. He did own many pieces of property here and there over the area north of the Republican River, roughly outlined by a triangle from Cambridge to Stockville to Indianola and back to Cambridge. He had loaned money to many people in that area. Once a year he came around to collect his money due on the loans and his rent on the lands he owned. He always walked unless some farmer gave him a ride in a wagon.

But Jansen never said much about where he was going or what his plans were. No one knew when he was going to call and ask for his money, so no one was even aware that he was missing until months after he had last been seen. Some neighbors happened to check with each other and discovered that the old man, who was in his seventies, had not been to some places he always visited.

Speculation was that he had decided to go to Omaha or Chicago or some other destination. He wouldn't have told anyone. He had last been seen in December of 1897. He had carried his little black bag in one hand as he walked. He never let it out of his

Brick schoolhouse, Cambridge, built in 1888
Nebraska, Our Towns

sight. People wondered how much money he carried in that bag. But no one found out.

It was April of 1898 before his son became worried. He wrote to his father infrequently and heard from him only once in a great while. Thomas Jansen was not one to waste his money on postage stamps. But when it had been nearly six months since L.H. Jansen had heard from his father, he began to inquire about him. He knew he had been in the Indianola-Stockville area in late '97.

The younger Jansen came to the area and began asking questions but found no clues as to the whereabouts of his father. So he hired a lawyer from Beatrice, A.H. Kidd, to launch an investigation. The lawyer began his investigation the first of June, 1898. He went back to the first of November, 1897, and found where Thomas Jansen had been in Topeka and followed him up into Nebraska. Kidd had no trouble following his trail into December. He was in Indianola on December 10.

There the trail apparently disappeared. The old man could have taken a train to some unknown destination. He could have just wandered off on foot, the way he always traveled, and disappeared into the winter. Or

something violent could have happened to him.

A check of the railroad depots brought no answers. No ticket agent recalled selling a ticket to the old man. It was beginning to look like he had wandered off, been struck by amnesia, or else had run afoul of some thief who would kill to get that black bag. The lawyer, Kidd, was not about to dismiss that last possibility.

Kidd then went to the hotels in the area and inquired if Jansen had taken a room there any time after December 10. The Leland Hotel in Indianola showed that Jansen had checked out there the morning of December 13. So Kidd was three days closer to the solution of the mystery. At the Cosgo Hotel, Jansen's name was on the list of diners that same day. More importantly, Mrs. Cosgo remembered that she had seen him with two other men in a wagon. She didn't notice where they went, but it was customary for Jansen to hitch a ride with someone in a wagon, so little interest had been taken when he left town.

Kidd backed up a few days and picked up Jansen's trail again. He had taken the stage from Stockville to Indianola on December 10. He had walked out to the farm of Mr. Messersmith and collected ninety-five dollars rent on the crop from the land he owned. Messersmith noted that the $95 went into the black bag he always carried.

Jansen had stopped at the Freedom post office and store. Freedom was a station on the stage line between Stockville and Bartley. The merchant and postmaster there was Frank Vernam. The next day found him at Andrew Hawkins' place where he collected money due on the mortgage he held on the place. From there he went to Bartley, then on to Indianola where he was last seen on December 13.

Nothing Kidd had found shed any light on what had happened to Thomas Jansen. He

The Carr sod house, east of
Indianola
Courtesy Evelyn Martin

The DeArmand Hotel at its peak
Nebraska, Our Towns

could find no trace of the wagon in which
Jansen had left Indianola. Who would
remember such a wagon and the driver?
There was nothing unusual about it.

Kidd talked to the sheriff of Frontier
County, E. L. Bradbury. Kidd's questions
around the country had roused the curiosity
of everyone. The sheriff was fielding too

many questions. Why wasn't he out trying to
find out what had happened? He agreed with
Kidd that a reward for information might
loosen some tongues.

Once more the investigator started where
Janson was last seen. He took a list of
everybody at the dinner at the Cosgo Hotel
that day noon. It was the next to last name

Believed to be the soddy on Andrew Hawkins' homestead
Courtesy Frontier County Museum

on the list that gave Kidd a clue. William Nixon had eaten there that day and he remembered talking to Jansen. Jansen had said he was going north of Indianola that afternoon to see a man named Nicholas Portz who lived four miles west of Freedom.

Kidd checked. Portz not only remembered Jansen but he recalled the day he was there, December 13. That was the day that Portz had sent his coyote and skunk hides to Funston's Fur House in St. Louis. Portz said that Jansen told him he was going home with Andy Hawkins to conclude some business.

Chris McKinney, a neighbor of Portz, confirmed that he saw Jansen with Andrew Hawkins and two other men in a wagon that afternoon. Kidd talked to the sheriff again. They decided if that was the last anyone had seen of Jansen, then Andrew Hawkins should be asked some questions. Sheriff Bradbury knew Hawkins, and knew he was a bit out of the ordinary, but he wouldn't expect him to do away with an old man for money. But who knew what a poor man might do to get wealth?

Andrew Hawkins was a short man, overweight, in his forties, and wore a black moustache. He was known to associate with the seamy side of life but was still a respectable neighbor.

When confronted with the fact that Kidd knew he had Jansen in his wagon that day in December, he admitted picking up the old man and giving him a ride. He said that Jansen was going toward Stockville, apparently to Messersmith's place. He said he let him out a few miles from his own place. He did admit he had a couple of men with him that day, Emory Conklin and Jesse Carrol.

Sheriff Bradbury was skeptical of Hawkins' story. Everything dovetailed with the things he had learned elsewhere, but he still felt that Hawkins was not telling everything. He and Kidd decided they should check on places where Hawkins might have spent the money, just in case he did steal what the old man had. Hawkins had very little money, and if he was spending a lot, it would be a basis for deeper investigation.

Hawkins and the two men with him that day, Carrol and Conklin, were all illiterate, poor farmers. Bradbury knew that Carrol and Conklin never had more than a few dollars at any time. Kidd and Bradbury began checking on every transaction any of the three had made after December 13.

They found that Hawkins had made a hundred dollars down payment on the land that Carrol had bought. And Hawkins had bought some land from A.Y. Lincoln and paid Lincoln $150 in cash. The two detectives were getting excited now.

They checked at Freedom with the merchant there, Frank Vernam. Vernam said that Hawkins had always paid cash for small amounts of anything he bought and charged larger items to be paid for when the crops came in. But recently he had been buying big things and paying cash for them, such as thirty dollars for a bicycle for his son and $22.50 for a sewing machine for his wife. Vernam said he'd seen the big roll of bills Hawkins had. Hawkins said he'd had a good

Main Street of early Indianola
Courtesy James Sughroue

Mrs. Van Pelt and her son, Robert, in front of her cafe, Stockville, 1915
Nebraska, Our Towns

Hill's Lunch Room and Bakery, Arapahoe
Nebraska, Our Towns

crop and his money came from that. No one else in the country had harvested a crop like that.

Hawkins paid an old doctor bill in Cambridge; bought a good team of horses in Stockville; and bought a buggy and cultivator in Bartley. In Arapahoe, they found evidence that Hawkins had bought another team of horses there. Suspicion was growing by leaps and bounds.

Still, there was no proof that Hawkins hadn't gotten his money honestly. He had raised eight hundred bushels of wheat in 1897 and sold it for fifty-five cents a bushel, and some corn at forty-four cents a bushel, as well as a dozen hogs at better than three dollars a hundredweight.

But Sheriff Bradbury wasn't satisfied. He was sure that Hawkins was the key to the mystery of Jensen's disappearance, but he had no solid proof. He decided to put an undercover man on the job. That man got a job in the harvest working for Hawkins.

Arapahoe landmark—octagon
house, built in 1872
Nebraska, Our Towns

But sometime after harvest, Hawkins fired his hired man. He told a neighbor, who asked why he fired such a good man, that he didn't trust the man. He was well educated, and an educated man wouldn't normally work at pitching bundles. He was sure he was some kind of detective, trying to find something bad about somebody in the neighborhood.

The detective had only one suspicious thing to report. He recommended that the sheriff investigate an old well about two miles north of Hawkins' house. The detective had heard some suspicious things about that well. Hawkins had spent part of the last winter filling that old well, which was 135 feet deep. He claimed it was a hazard to livestock. He had been filling it with old hay and manure.

The sheriff did go to look at the well. It was filled with hay and manure as the detective had said. That certainly was not what most people used to fill a well. This would rot away and leave a hole just as hazardous to livestock as the open well had been.

The sheriff inquired around and confirmed that it had been Hawkins who had filled the well last winter. The only logical excuse for using hay and manure would be that the ground was frozen and he couldn't dig up

dirt to put in the well. But why had he been in such a hurry to fill it that he couldn't wait till spring?

Sheriff Bradbury started inquiring, and found neighbors who had seen Andy Hawkins hauling hay and manure to the old well last winter. Then the sheriff happened to question A.Y. Lincoln, who had owned that piece of land where the well was before Hawkins bought it. Lincoln recalled that he had driven through that valley last winter before he sold the land. He had some hay to check there. He recalled seeing wagon tracks veering off the road over close to the well then back to the road. He thought little about it then. Often people who had some junk to dispose of would throw it down an abandoned well someplace.

That bit of knowledge made the sheriff reach a decision. He got some men to help him, and they proceeded to the well and began digging out the hay and manure. It was a monumental job, since the well was 135 feet deep. It was four feet wide, so that hole contained a lot of material.

It was slow work. Carrol happened by on his way to work with a threshing crew, the same crew that included Hawkins. The sheriff questioned the man who bossed the threshing crew. He said that Hawkins and Carrol had held a conference that afternoon. Hawkins didn't appear for work the next morning. Some said he had gone to McCook on business. Investigation showed that he had gone to talk to a lawyer. Since he wasn't accused of anything yet, this move only strengthened the sheriff's conviction that Hawkins had something to hide.

After another day's work, they finally got to the bottom of the well. There they found the body of a man jammed head first into the mud. A coroner's jury was quickly assembled. The body, covered with the hay and manure, was well preserved, considering how long it had been there. Identification was simple and quick. It was the body of Thomas Jansen. His watch, ring and money pouch were gone. His shoes were off his feet and the coroner's jury speculated that the murderer had removed the shoes, hoping to find additional money hidden there. A fracture at the base of the skull told how Jansen had died. He hadn't accidentally fallen into the well.

Andrew Hawkins was arrested and charged with the murder. He simply said that he knew nothing about it. He said he had filled the well because it was a hazard to livestock. He had paid for the things he bought with the money he got from his good crop in 1897.

Looking for convincing evidence, the prosecuting attorneys found that Mrs. Carrol had been asked to wash a blood-stained blanket for Hawkins, but the blanket had disappeared. The attorney found two men who said they had heard Hawkins say he was going to "knock off" the old man if he didn't stop badgering him for his interest payments. Jansen had owned a mortgage on Hawkins' place, and Hawkins claimed he didn't have the money to pay the interest.

They went to court in Stockville on December 12, 1898, with a load of circumstantial evidence, but no confession

The well down which Hawkins threw Thomas Jansen's body after he killed him
Courtesy Frontier County Museum

Senator George Norris, when he lived in Beaver City
Nebraska, Our Towns

from Hawkins. Hawkins still insisted he knew nothing about the whole affair.

What little defense Hawkins' attorneys could produce had little effect on the jury. Ten days after the trial began, on December 22, the jury brought in a verdict of guilty of murder in the first degree.

Sheriff Bradbury's suspicions of Hawkins and what he might do focused on the prisoner just before sentence was pronounced. He led the prisoner out of the courtroom and searched him. He found a loaded .38 calibre pistol hidden in his pocket. What he intended to do with it was not disclosed.

Judge George W. Norris pronounced the sentence of life imprisonment and most who heard the trial felt it was a just sentence.

Frontier County Courthouse, where Hawkins was tried
Courtesy Frontier County Museum

BIBLIOGRAPHY

BOOKS

Andreas, A. T. *History of Nebraska*. Chicago: Western History Collection, 1882.
Bang, Roy E. *Heroes Without Medals—A Pioneer History of Kearney County*. Minden, Nebraska: Warp Publishing Co., 1952.
Bridgeport Lion's Club. *A Century or Two Ago*.
Chase County History. *Volume II*. Champion, Nebraska: Chase County Historical Society, 1965.
Haymart, Laura. *A Collection of Early Giltner Stories*. Hastings, Nebraska: Cornhusker Press.
O'Gara, W. H. *In All Its Fury*. Lincoln, Nebraska: Dorothy Jenkins, 1975.
Sheldon, Addison E. *History and Stories of Nebraska*. Chicago: University Publishing Co., 1913.
Sherard, Gerald E. *Historical Sketches of Giltner, Nebraska*. Baltimore: Gateway Press, 1985.
Wanek, Winnie Lewis. *Historical Account of the Murder of William Lewis*.

MAGAZINES

City of Curtis Records.
Lowe, Bert. "Carns."
Tales of Pioneer Days
Vernam, Glenn. "Wagon Road to Death." *Frontier Times*.

NEWSPAPERS

Beatrice Daily Sun. August 3, 1891; April 29, 1905.
Beatice Daily Sun. 1957 Centennial Edition.
The Beatrice Express. August 3, 1891.
Cambridge Monitor. December 1884.
The Daily Nebraska State Journal, Lincoln. March 26, 1887.
Daily State Journal. Lincoln, Nebraska. December 18, 1884; December 21, 1884.
Farnham Gazette. December 2, 1893; 50th Anniversary Edition, 1936.
Frontier County Faber. Stockville, Nebraska. December, 1884.
Lexington Pioneer. 1936.
Lincoln State Journal. April 20, 1894.
McCook Daily Gazette. July 16, 1965.
Omaha Bee. June 1, 1889; June 2, 1889.
Omaha Herald. May 2, 1876; December 26, 1880.
Omaha Republican. June 2, 1889; March 21, 1890.
Omaha Sunday Bee. January 10, 1926.
Springview Herald. January 24, 1935.

IV

COMING OF AGE

1900–1926

Coming Of Age

Turning the corner from the Nineteenth Century to the Twentieth Century didn't guarantee that the old ways of settling arguments with gun or knife would automatically fade into the gentle, peaceful life of Utopia.

The urge to use the rope for quick, sure justice was supposedly gone but the threat reared its head occasionally even in the "civilized" age in which men lived.

Nor was brutality eliminated. Consider the Puls murder in Frontier County in 1903. Few murders in the preceding century exceeded it in savagery.

Centuries may come and centuries may go, but man seems to go on forever without a great deal of change in his methods of getting what he wants, regardless of the wants and needs of others. He seems to be quick to turn to violence and slow to learn that it never pays.

The first quarter of the Twentieth Century had its full share of examples of mankind's brutality to man, and Nebraska claimed its little corner in those statistics. Here are a few samples of how Nebraska fared from 1900 to 1926.

Puls Murder—Frontier County   1903

Aerial view of Eustis in 1919

Charles Frymire was taken into the home of his uncle and aunt, the W.D. Frymires, near Eustis, Nebraska, when he was very small. The Frymires had no children of their own, and they thought this was the opportunity to bring up a boy who would take care of them in their old age. But Charles Frymire had a streak in him that his uncle hadn't expected, and had no way of handling.

As Charles got older, he began to seek ways of getting what he wanted when he didn't deserve it. When the new teacher came to teach the local school district, Frymire, grown now, decided he wanted her—but she had no time for him. Her name was Theresa (often called Tracy) Oldenburg and she had eyes only for another young man, Richard Puls.

That didn't deter Charles Frymire. He had read a little in law books and had come across an old law of obsolete York state about contract marriages. He wrote up a copy of that contract and took it to Theresa and, at the point of a gun, made her sign it. He would have his way. Theresa was completely

consumed by fear of Frymire. He threatened to kill her if she ever told anyone about the contract. He held her to the terms of the contract she had signed but never let anyone in the neighborhood know about it.

In her second term teaching the school, she boarded with the B.E. Woods family. Somehow she got her hands on the contract and burned it. At last, she was free. But when she told Frymire that the contract was destroyed and he learned that it really was, he went after Woods where Theresa stayed. He promised Woods that he would come in Saturday and kill him if Woods didn't kill him first. Woods made arrangements to be sure that if anyone died, it would be Frymire.

But things developed in the meantime that pushed Frymire's revenge against Woods out of his mind. On Thursday, Theresa and Richard Puls were married at the church in town. Frymire didn't hear about it until he got to town on Saturday. He was furious. He called a neighbor, named Heater, into a conference in the store and his plan began to take shape.

Frymire borrowed Heater's buggy and

soon left town with it. He went first to Oelkers place, who were apparently Theresa's special friends, thinking she might be there. She wasn't and he demanded to know where she was. Oelkers said the couple were in their own home. Frymire pulled his gun and warned the Oelkers not to leave their place or he'd shoot them. He waved his gun and told them this was what Theresa was going to get.

Then he drove toward the place where the Oelkers had said the new Mr. and Mrs. Puls were living. He stopped the buggy some distance from the house and tied the team. Then he walked quietly toward the house. The couple inside had not yet discovered they had company. The first they knew of his presence was the moment he fired two shots through the window. Neither shot hit its target but Richard Puls quickly locked the door and the couple dashed into the back room.

Frymire reached the door, found it locked, and proceeded to kick it in. Then he charged into the back room and began shooting. One bullet hit Theresa in the abdomen. Reports said that his second shot at Richard Puls was a dud. The hammer clicked but the gun didn't fire. Puls grappled with Frymire, and it was a vicious fight for a few moments until Frymire got in some hard licks to the head with his gun. Puls was put out of the fight, unconscious.

Then Frymire grabbed Theresa where she was lying on the floor, and threw her out into the yard. Following her through the door, he jumped on her, smashing her with his boots. She screamed and begged him to kill her. But he shouted, "No!" He said death was too good for her; he wanted to see her suffer.

In his frenzy, he stomped her again and again, then grabbed her and dragged her to the buggy. Richard regained consciousness and staggered out into the yard. Frymire threatened him with the gun and told him he'd shoot him if he tried to follow them.

Frymire shoved Theresa into the buggy, then climbed in himself and drove off. Puls got his horse and rode to town to file a complaint before Justice Pinch, charging Frymire with attempted murder. A warrant was issued for Frymire's arrest and given to Constable Haynes. Haynes and his brother rode out of town at top speed.

In the meantime, Frymire began to come out of his frenzy. Theresa was in such screaming pain from her wound and the stomping Frymire had given her that he

The water tower replaced the windmill in Eustis
Nebraska, Our Towns

stopped as they were passing the school house and took her inside. Then Frymire drove wildly on to Oelkers, but the two older members of the family were gone. Frymire sent the younger brother of Richard Puls, who was at the Oelkers place, to town to get a doctor. Then he took Minnie Oelkers back to the school house with him.

They found Theresa in such bad shape that they carried her to the Oelkers house where they could try to ease the pain. While Minnie worked with the wounded girl, Frymire sat back and watched.

That was where Constable Haynes found Frymire, arrested him, and took him back to town. By eleven o'clock that night, he was standing before Justice pinch. Pinch was shocked at what Constable Haynes told him, and he told Haynes to hold Frymire under tight security until ten o'clock Monday morning, when there would be a formal hearing.

There wasn't much of a jail at Eustis, so Haynes hired two guards to help him watch Frymire. The sheriff and the county attorney were notified, and they came to Eustis on Sunday morning to take charge of the prisoner.

At the hearing, Frymire demanded to be taken to the county seat; so they left at noon for Stockville. When the story of his contract marriage came out, fury gripped most of the community. But there was pity, too—mostly for Theresa and her new husband—Richard Puls, and for Mr. and Mrs. W.D. Frymire, who had tried hard to raise Charles right. Their disappointment had to be acute.

The doctors had done what they could for Theresa, including an operation to remove the bullet. But they couldn't find it. It was the tromping as much as the bullet wound that caused Theresa to gradually sink away. On Thursday morning, she died.

Theresa Puls' funeral was on Saturday, February 28, in the same church where she and Richard Puls had been married barely a week before.

Charles Frymire's trial came up in district court that fall in early October. Many could not understand how the jury could bring in a verdict of manslaughter when to most people, it was an outright case of murder in the first degree.

The Phoenix Pharmacy,
Stockville, 1925
Nebraska, Our Towns

Judge Orr gave Frymire the ultimate sentence for manslaughter, ten years in prison at hard labor. Each year on February 21, the anniversary of his shooting and trampling of Theresa Puls, he would spend in solitary confinement. Those who heard the sentence felt that the judge would have made the sentence much more severe if the jury had not limited him by its verdict.

McCullough Murder—
Adams County   1906

1900 didn't mean that the days of violence were over in Hastings. A jolt of that violence came from what was almost a native son. Bonde Pearson came from Sweden in 1872 when he was only four years old and grew up on a farm about ten miles southeast of Hastings.

As soon as he was grown he headed west, and when he came back to Hastings, he had changed. He was now Barney Pearson, and he'd never go back to his given name of Bonde. He also had a wife, having married Sarah Thrifty (Tifty) in Pueblo, Colorado, in 1891. There was a daughter now, Mildred.

Barney Pearson
Courtesy Adams County Historical Society

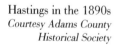

Hastings in the 1890s
*Courtesy Adams County
Historical Society*

In Pueblo, he had driven the town's fire horses. His love of horses had put him in the business of buying wild horses caught up off the range, mainly in Wyoming, and shipping them back to farming and ranching areas and selling them.

When he got back to Hastings, he continued with this business. He made many trips to Wyoming to buy unbroken horses. It was on an aborted trip to Cheyenne when he got into deep trouble. He got only as far as Grand Island and, for some reason, decided to come back home.

It was late Saturday night when he arrived home. He found that his wife had taken the opportunity of his absence to stage a party. Barney and Sarah had not been getting along well at all but he hadn't expected anything like this.

It was past midnight when he got to his house at 109 East Fifth Street and found the party still in progress. If there had been many at the party, most of them apparently had left. The one party-goer that irked Barney was Walter McCullough (McCulluy). Though no mention of McCullough is made before this night, it was obviously not the first time something like this had happened. Barney was furious. He went first to a minister, Reverend Lemkau, and asked him to go and look into Pearson's house and see what was going on. The minister was reluctant to pry into other peoples' affairs but Barney Pearson insisted.

Pearson was carrying his shotgun when he called on the minister. Lemkau said later he thought that Barney intended to use the shotgun to help arrest the intruder in his house.

At the railroad tracks, Barney stopped and insisted that Lemkau go on and see what was happening in Pearson's house. The minister made the trip but the curtain over the window was drawn and he quickly retreated to the tracks. Barney, however, was gone.

About that time, Lemkau heard the report of a shotgun. He decided Barney had fired his gun in the air to frighten the people inside his house.

A minute later a man came out of the house without hat or coat but that was not alarming. It was about 12:30 AM, July 29, and not cold enough to need a coat. The man saw Lemkau and asked who he was. Then he told him that he had been shot. The minister walked down the street with the man without knowing his identity. But after a short distance, the man appeared too weak to go on so the minister left him on the doorstep of a neighbor of Barney Pearson and ran home to call the police.

M.A. Hartigan, who lived in the house where the wounded man had stopped, heard some pounding on the front porch and went to investigate. He found Walter McCullough on the porch in weak condition from loss of blood. Hartigan called the police and a doctor.

Upon examining the patient, the doctor realized the seriousness of the wound and McCullough, notified of that, asked that his wife be brought. McCullough talked to his wife a while, but he said very little after that.

Another doctor was called in and the two operated on the victim, but it was obvious that their skills could not repair the damage done by the shotgun.

Police checked the Pearson house, saw where the window had been broken by the shotgun blast. Mrs. Pearson could give them no clues as to who might have shot her companion. The Pearsons had no enemies, she said. Her husband was in Wyoming buying horses.

But the police soon found out differently concerning Barney Pearson's buying trip. They found Barney at his parents' home on East Fifth Street, where the elder Pearsons had retired after leaving the farm where Barney had been brought up. The police arrested Barney and took him to jail.

A day later Walter McCullough died, and the original charge against Barney of shooting with the intent to kill was dismissed and a new charge of murder was filed. The hearing set for the first day of August was put off until the 4th of August to give the defense attorney time to organize his defense.

Barney Pearson appeared in court that morning, cleanly dressed and as calm as if he were a spectator. He did make the remark that he couldn't see why the state was prosecuting him. He felt that the state ought to be defending him, considering the circumstances.

The trial began four months later on December 7, 1906. Barney had been facing a divorce suit filed by his wife before the shooting incident took place. Barney would not contest the divorce but he did ask his attorney to make sure his daughter, Millie, went to a good school. She should be separated from her mother, he insisted.

The trial, attended by huge crowds, ended in a hung jury. The second trial, held on May 7, 1907, brought a verdict of not guilty. Acquitted from any guilt in the killing of Walter McCullough, Barney went on to blaze a flamboyant trail across Nebraska and other states until his death in 1942.

Eaffley Murder—Knox County 1909

In the Taxwell Billiard Hall in Bloomington, a quarrel, if it could be called a quarrel, was pushed too far. It was Friday, February 12, 1909.

Two young men, neither married yet, were in the hall. Herman Sorey was watching the games, not looking for trouble. Mike Eaffley was looking for what he called fun. He obviously was the kind who loved to push those around who didn't push back. He underestimated Herman Sorey.

According to witnesses, Eaffley had been unusually quarrelsome that day and had bothered several customers in the billiard hall and restaurant. Herman Sorey had come to Bloomington from Missouri Valley, Iowa, and this day was tending to his own business. Eaffley discovered that he was one he could push around and get no opposition.

Eaffley tried to get an argument out of Sorey, but Sorey wasn't inclined to argue. Eaffley pushed Sorey back against the wall and slapped him a couple of times, swearing at him. Still Sorey wouldn't fight back.

When Eaffley backed off, Sorey made an attempt to get out the door but Eaffley blocked the doorway, slapping him a couple more times. Sorey warned him to let him alone or he'd use his knife on him. He actually pulled the knife out.

The restaurant owner hurried over and separated the two young men and told them both to simmer down. They seemed to obey and things got quiet again.

But Eaffley was not satisfied. He went after Sorey again, swearing at him and slapping him on both sides of the head, pushing him back against the wall.

Nobody saw Sorey pull his knife out this time. The first they realized he had used the knife was when Eaffley staggered back and yelled, "I'm stabbed. Send for a doctor."

Eaffley fell to the floor and, before anyone could get a doctor, he died. Sorey was immediately arrested. A coroner's jury rendered the verdict that Mike Eaffley had died from a knife wound inflicted by Herman Sorey.

Sorey had a preliminary hearing before Judge Barge, who heard reports from several eye witnesses to the trouble in the hall. Then he bound Sorey over to the district court, setting his bond at two thousand dollars. Sorey had no trouble raising the bond money.

It was the general opinion of those who had seen the entire scuffle that Sorey had acted in self defense. Most men would have

Bloomington Mills,
Franklin County
Nebraska, Our Towns

struck back sooner than Sorey had, but likely not with a knife in the heart.

It was Bloomington's first murder.

Waithers Murder—Clay County   1909

Most murder victims are killed by gunshot wounds or blows from a hard blunt object. Peter Waithers was killed by a hard blunt object, if you can call a fist such an instrument.

The fight took place at the home of John Karney on the border of Clay and Adams Counties southeast of Hastings. John Karney's family had scarlet fever. Peter Waithers belonged to the board of supervisors and he was approached by Dr. Bailey, after the doctor had been out to Karney's house to post a quarantine to try to halt the spread of the disease. John Karney took a very dim view of a quarantine that would keep him and all his family confined to their farm until the disease had run its course through all the family. He refused to let the doctor post the quarantine notice. So, Dr. Bailey had called on Peter Waithers for help. In another report, the disease being quarantined was said to be diphtheria.

When the doctor and Peter Waithers arrived at the Karney farm, they found Mr. Karney of the same opinion that Dr. Bailey had discovered earlier. Peter Waithers insisted that the quarantine must be put on the home to protect the rest of the community. In just a matter of a minute, John Karney and Peter Waithers were in a fist fight to prove that might made right. Karney got the better of the fight, knocking Waithers down with a hard blow to the jaw.

The doctor and Waithers went back to Glenville, but a few days later Peter Waithers suddenly became paralyzed over part of his body. Even then, it was a couple of days before they brought him to the sanitarium in Hastings.

The first report after the fight was Waithers had suffered a broken jaw in the fight. Later it was discovered that the jaw was not broken but a blood vessel in his brain had been ruptured. He died on Friday, October 8, 1909.

John Karney was arrested and held in custody until the coroner's report was made. The coroner's jury didn't say definitely that the injury from the fight was the cause of Waithers' death, but there was no sign of any other injury that could have caused it. After the inquest, Karney was charged with second degree murder. But due to the inconclusive report of the coroner's jury, it wasn't likely that Karney could be convicted on the charge.

Newell Murder—Adams County   1910

Just a few months after the Waithers killing, a murder in a pool room on North Hastings Avenue made the headlines in the *Hastings Daily Tribune* for several days. On Wednesday afternoon, February 16, 1910, Arthur Anderson, a black man about twenty years old, was playing a game of billiards with Henry Wienas. Arthur Newell, a white man a little younger than Anderson, was watching.

It was apparent that the two young men had been needling each other before. Newell made some remarks about Anderson's playing and Anderson told him to keep out of this game. Newell had a file, and he made a grinning remark that he would file off Anderson's nose.

They tossed a few more jibes at each other and the others around the room thought it was all in fun. Anderson even made a pass at Newell with his billiard cue but he was grinning when he did it.

Then it happened. Not even those who saw it could believe it. Arthur Anderson suddenly swung his billiard cue with all his strength and hit Arthur Newell on the side of the head. Newell slumped forward and fell off the bench. Anderson looked at him a

Denver House in Hastings

Courtesy Adams County Historical Society

Billiard Hall, where Arthur Newell
was killed, in Hastings
*Courtesy Adams County
Historical Society*

moment then removed his apron which he used while working at the Hughes Restaurant. Putting on his coat, he left the pool room. Everyone in the room seemed stunned by the sudden outburst of violence and did nothing to stop him from leaving.

When they recovered enough to rush to Newell to see how badly he was hurt, Anderson was gone. Newell was dead. The cue had cut a gash along his temple. The coroner's report later said, "The bones on the lower floor of the brain had been shattered."

As soon as the people realized the seriousness of the affair, they rushed out to notify police and to try to catch the killer. There was a policeman on his beat right across from the billiard hall and he had seen Anderson leave the hall and go hurriedly down the street. But by the time someone had told him what had happened, Anderson was nowhere in sight.

The sheriff, his deputies, and the police hurriedly organized a search for the killer. They found plenty of people who had seen a Negro walking down the street, and once out on the railroad tracks, but none of these sightings helped the officers catch up with the fugitive.

On the next day after the murder, rumors flashed over town from every direction. Some said Anderson had hidden in a culvert and

had been found and brought in. Another rumor said he had been arrested some distance from town and brought in, but the police emphatically denied it. The rumor mill said that the denial was just to prevent a lynch mob from forming. Lynch talk was rampant everywhere.

But the police posted a reward of $250 for information leading to the arrest of Arthur Anderson. That put to rest some of the rumors that Anderson was already in custody. The police put out a detailed description of the killer, including the fact that he was wearing a light gray suit, tennis shoes, black Stetson hat, and black overcoat.

Following every tip they received, the police probed haystacks, searched barns and vacant buildings, and went through every outgoing train. But they found no trace of Arthur Anderson.

Actually, Anderson had hidden in a culvert that first day and came out about eight o'clock to visit two black families he knew. One allowed him to warm his feet, which were protected from the mid-February cold only by tennis shoes. As soon as he was gone, the family telephoned the police, but when they arrived, Anderson had disappeared again.

The hunt continued through the cold days until Saturday, three days after the murder in the pool room. That was the day of Arthur Newell's funeral. About noon on that day a farmer drove into Glenville, a short distance southeast of Hastings in the western edge of Clay County, and reported seeing a black man by a little fire near the railroad tracks. Men from Glenville quickly went out that way and found Arthur Anderson sitting by a small fire he had started, trying to warm himself. He offered no resistance when he was arrested. He was weak from three days without food or water and his feet were frozen. The weather had been cold and he'd been hiding in a pile of railroad ties since the first night after the murder.

The sheriff in Hastings had already been alerted that Anderson was down near Glenville. Anderson, almost starved, had finally gone to the home of Lewis Norton, close to his hiding place, and asked for food. It had been given to him and Norton had watched where he went with it. Then he telephoned the sheriff in Hastings. But before the sheriff could get ready to leave, he got a call that farmers near Glenville had captured Anderson and were holding him until the sheriff could get there. Anderson's big fear was of being lynched, not being arrested.

Anderson was paying dearly for his seventy hours of exposure after he escaped from the pool room Wednesday afternoon. His feet were frozen solid well up above his ankles. His overcoat had protected his body fairly well but the tennis shoes had been little protection for his feet.

He was arraigned Monday morning but they had to carry him to the court room in a chair. The trial would be postponed until something was done about his feet.

By the next day, the doctors decided there was no chance of saving Anderson's feet so both were amputated. When his leg stumps had sufficiently healed, he was brought into court for trial. There the prosecuting attorney agreed to a five year sentence to save the

court the cost of a trial. The defense agreed and Arthur Anderson was sentenced to five years in the penitentiary at hard labor. It was not explained how he could do much hard labor with no feet to stand on. But some felt that he had already paid part of the price for his murder of Arthur Newell by losing his feet, which was a direct result of his attempt to avoid being caught and punished for his crime.

Hodges Murder—Adams County   1910

Only a few months after the Newell murder, another fight at Kenesaw, just west of Hastings in Adams County, made the news. It seemed to have little more provocation than the fight in the pool room in Hastings, but the results were just as serious.

Roy Hodges had been the editor of the *Kenesaw Citizen* for a while but, at age twenty-six, had stepped down from that job. Roy's aunt ran a boarding house in Kenesaw and Roy was there for supper on the eve of the Fourth of July. One of the boarders, a man named Frank Etue (Eaton in some reports) was also at supper there. When the meal was finished, Etue, who apparently had made previous arrangements with Mrs. Belle Hodges who operated the boarding house, to charge the meal, made the remark as he left the table to "put it on ice."

Roy Hodges took exception to that and told Etue to pay for his meal or he'd take it out of his hide. This apparently infuriated Etue and he hit Hodges, according to one report, and knocked him out of his chair and against the wall. Within seconds, they were fighting like two school boys. Other boarders separated the two and Hodges went outside. From there, he challenged Etue to come outside, too, and finish the fight.

Etue was several years older than Hodges but he accepted the challenge and went outside. The fight resumed with a vengeance

Kenesaw depot
Courtesy Marie Olsen

Main Street in early Kenesaw
Courtesy Marie Olsen

and Roy Hodges was getting the better of it. They were in a clinch when suddenly Etue pulled a revolver from his pocket and fired it.

The first shot hit Hodges in the elbow, the second in the knee. That threw Hodges back on the ground. According to the boarders who came out to witness the fight, Etue's third shot was fired at Hodges after he was flat on his back on the ground. That shot hit the ex-editor in the abdomen.

Etue turned then and climbed into a buggy at the hitchrack and started out of town, but some of the witnesses to the fight stopped the team. Etue jumped out of the buggy and began running but a man named Roy Case caught him and turned him over to the marshal in town. The marshal delivered him to the sheriff in Hastings.

On the sixth of July, three days after the shooting, Roy Hodges was still hanging on so the decision was made to bring him to Hastings to the Nebraska Sanitarium where he could get better care. The bullets had been removed from his arm and his knee but nothing had been done about the bullet in his abdomen.

The next morning, the seventh of July, Frank Etue was officially charged with shooting Hodges with intent to kill. No bail was set because Etue had no means of raising security, regardless of the amount.

On the morning of July 8, Roy Hodges died of poisoning from the bullet wound in his abdomen. The charge against Etue was changed from intent to kill to murder.

A side issue arose before the preliminary

hearing for Etue. It involved the news that the reason Roy Hodges hadn't received an operation to remove the bullet in his abdomen and repair the interior damage was because Hodges had no money to pay for the operation, and the doctor's request to the county for the guarantee of hospital payment was refused.

At the time of the hearing Etue still showed the physical signs of his fight with Roy Hodges. His eye was black and there were cuts on his lip and face. Those injuries were all healed by the time of his trial on September 27.

The lawyers for the prosecution and defense had gotten together and tried to reach a compromise. There was no doubt of Etue's guilt. His punishment was the sticker. The prosecution wanted ten years; the defense was willing to allow five years. Before the trial came into court, they had agreed on a compromise of seven-and-a-half years in the penitentiary. Judge Duncan agreed and issued that sentence, thus saving the county the cost of a trial.

Flege Murder—Dixon County 1912

In 1912, William Flege and his sister owned and worked a farm in northeastern Nebraska. They didn't agree much of the time on the way the farm was operated.

William Flege loved cars and had bought one for himself. After he got it, he was on the road more than he was on the farm. His sister was determined that he should work more on the farm. They couldn't make money while he was running around in his car.

They hired a young German, named Eightencamp, to work on the farm. Apparently William felt that would give him much more liberty to be away from the farm and its work. That wasn't the way his sister saw it. They quarreled frequently and often furiously.

At one of those bitter quarrels, William grabbed a pistol and shot his sister, killing her almost instantly. Eightencamp was a witness to that argument, but Flege threatened to kill him if he ever said a word about it to anyone. Eightencamp held his tongue when questions were asked.

William Flege was arrested and charged with first degree murder. Before the trial, young Eightencamp was put under extreme pressure to tell what he had seen. Though he denied seeing anything, the authorities were sure he had. He finally broke down and

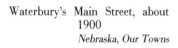

Waterbury's Main Street, about 1900
Nebraska, Our Towns

confessed that he had seen the quarrel that ended in William Flege shooting his sister. But he had been threatened with death if he told, so he had gone back to the field where he had been working and stayed there until after the authorities had been out and the excitement had died down.

The testimony was enough to convince the jury. William Flege was convicted and sentenced to life imprisonment. His lawyers worked on the case, trying to get another trial on the basis that the original jury had been given the wrong instructions. People wondered what instructions could have been wrong after Eightencamp told his story. There was little doubt among those who heard him that he was telling exactly what he had seen.

Jewett Murder—
Washington County   1913

George Jewett was a travelling salesman when he married in Creighton, Knox County, and settled down. A baby girl was born to the couple but they had no intention of keeping the child. The infant was born on July 8, 1913, and the father agreed to take the child to Omaha.

A nurse went along with Jewett on his trip to Omaha to deliver the baby to an orphanage or to someone who was waiting to care for it. Even the nurse seemed uncertain about the true destination of the baby.

They took a car from Creighton to Plainview and there they boarded a train and went to Omaha. They spent the night in the Paxton Hotel and the next morning, Jewett took the baby and started for the home that was to take care of the baby, leaving the nurse behind.

As he started down the stairs in the hotel, the baby cried. Jewett apparently did not want to be seen carrying a baby so he returned to the room where the nurse put the baby in his grip, a small valise. The nurse made the baby comfortable there and made Jewett promise to keep the grip open so the baby would have plenty of air.

Jewett left the hotel, carefully carrying the grip with the baby. The nurse, in her testimony, said she didn't see the baby again.

Authorities found a dead baby along the railroad right-of-way near Arlington later

Public school at Creighton
Courtesy Nebraska State Historical Society

Depot at Arlington, Washington County. The Jewett baby was found near here.
Nebraska, Our Towns

Railroad cars on a track, like the one where the Jewett baby was found murdered
Courtesy Kansas State Historical Society

that day, and it was identified as the Jewett baby; only a couple of days old.

George Jewett was found back in Creighton where he had told his wife that the baby was doing fine in its new home in Omaha. But the baby had not arrived at any home in Omaha, and George Jewett couldn't explain that. He was arrested and charged with first degree murder.

He asked for bail to be set but the court refused. Bail could not be allowed to prisoners charged with first degree murder.

Jewett appealed to the State Supreme Court but the same law applied there. George Jewett would have to stay in jail in Washington County, where the dead baby was found, until his trial. Murderers of babies were not held in any higher esteem than murderers of adults.

Layton Murder— Scottsbluff County 1915

On the night of June 11, 1915, Joseph Layton was sitting in the living room of his

Courthouse and Jail Rocks, downstream from Scottsbluff

Courtesy Nebraska State Historical Society

father-in-law, Dan Jordon, reading, when a bullet came through the window and struck him, killing him almost instantly.

The immediate story that came out was that the Jordon family, including Dan Jordon and his wife, their daughter, who was Joseph Layton's wife, and the maid, an eighteen-year-old girl, were sitting in the room with Layton when he was killed.

The sheriff came out and investigated the crime but did nothing until after Layton's funeral. Then he shocked the neighbors by arresting Dan Jordon, Layton's father-in-law.

Jordon denied the charge and stuck to his story that he was sitting in the room with his son-in-law when the shot was fired through the window. The sheriff questioned the maid and she corroborated Jordon's statement.

The sheriff could find no suspects in the neighborhood who had any reason to sneak in and kill Layton. He did find that Dan Jordon had come from the mountains of California and he had a bad reputation there. So his suspicions of Jordon remained.

Finding a motive for the murder took a little more digging, but he finally settled on the fact that Layton had quite a bit of property and Jordon's daughter would be wealthy if Layton was dead.

Jordon then pointed out that Joseph

C.B.&Q. Depot, Scottsbluff
*Courtesy Nebraska State
Historical Society*

Layton had gotten into an argument with a young Russian employee on his farm some time before and struck him with a shovel. That blow had resulted in the Russian's death but Layton was not convicted of the murder. At the time of the shot through the window, Jordon said that Mrs. Jordon and her daughter had run into the pantry screaming that the Russians were shooting. Dan Jordon argued that was proof that some Russian friend of the man Layton had hit with the shovel had gotten his revenge by shooting Layton.

The sheriff could find no one who would fit the role of the avenger. He still believed the theory that Jordon was trying to enrich his daughter by killing her husband. He checked everything carefully. He finally found the proof that he thought he needed. There were footprints just outside the window where the killer had stood when he fired the shot. Dan Jordon's shoes fit those prints exactly.

He again questioned the girl who worked at the Jordon's. Under pressure, she finally changed her story and admitted that she was not in the room and did not see Jordon there when Layton was killed. But Dan Jordon had told her so often that he was there that she had said he was.

With Jordon in jail, the sheriff looked for the gun. Jordon said he didn't own a gun, but a long search finally brought a gun to light. It was hidden deep in the hay in the mow of the barn. It had one shot fired from the cylinder and the remaining cartridges in the gun were the explosive bullets just like the one that had killed Layton. Buried in an outhouse, the sheriff and his deputies found several more shells that fit the revolver they'd found in the haymow.

Working on the theory that Jordon was trying to enrich his daughter by killing her husband, he arrested Mrs. Layton, too, as a conspirator in the crime. But at the preliminary hearing, she was dismissed. There wasn't any evidence that she had anything to do with the killing.

At the trial, the evidence was presented and Jordon's defense could not destroy it.

Jordon was convicted of murder and sentenced to life imprisonment. An appeal was made to the state supreme court but the general feeling among those who had attended the trial was that Dan Jordon had received a fair trial and had also been given a just sentence.

Tuttle Murder—
Scottsbluff County   1916

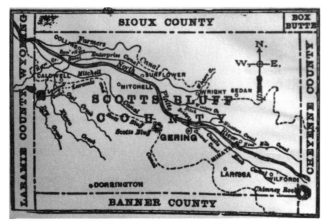

Scottsbluff County map, used in 1892
Nebraska, Our Towns

Trouble festered through the day on July 31, 1916, and finally erupted in violence that evening. Clifford and Margaret Tuttle had been married ten years before, but had quarreled much of their time together. Margaret had been only about fifteen when they were married. They had moved to Scottsbluff about a year before the tragic day. Their quarrels had finally ended in divorce.

Clifford Tuttle had gone to Alliance and Omaha to work while Margaret had done other things. She had been gone from Scottsbluff for a while before the fateful day. Both had returned to Scottsbluff about the same time.

The couple were seen together several times that day and were quarreling most of the time. Margaret said she had loaned

Clifford some money when he left and she wanted him to pay it back. That only led to another quarrel.

After dinner, they had a quarrel near the bandstand in the park and he was heard to tell her, "Hop to it, Old Girl," apparently in response to some statement or threat she had made. They quarreled again after supper. Then they took a walk around the block. At the corner of Third and Pawnee Streets, the arguments ended in two pistol shots that put Clifford Tuttle down to stay.

Those near enough to hear the shots and see the flash of the revolver in the twilight rushed to the scene. They found Margaret sitting on the walk with her husband's head in her lap. She readily admitted that she had shot him.

Tuttle's body was carried to the Crawford Garage and then taken from there by Coroner F.A. McCleary to the morgue. Margaret was arrested and quietly went to Gering to the county jail there.

Clifford Tuttle's funeral was held on Thursday, August 3. He was twenty-nine years old. His sister who lived in Scottsbluff, his father from Grand Island, and a brother from Omaha were the chief mourners.

Margaret Tuttle was brought up for a preliminary hearing on August 16. She was charged with first degree murder and pled not guilty. The witnesses who were called agreed on what they saw and heard. Judge DeLaMatter ordered her bound over to the district court without bail.

The trial came up in February of 1917. On February 27, the trial got under way after a jury had been selected and opening statements gotten out of the way. The plea of Margaret Tuttle was self defense. The state promised to show that it was premeditated murder.

The prosecution had many witnesses lined up while the defense had only a few. The prosecution brought out the same witnesses

Broadway Street, Scottsbluff, 1926
Courtesy Nebraska State Historical Society

who had testified at the preliminary hearing which resulted in Margaret Tuttle being charged with murder. Those witnesses testified that they heard the shots and saw Clifford Tuttle fall. None could say exactly what happened immediately before the shots.

When the defense got its turn, Margaret Tuttle was called to the stand. She told her story simply. She said she had asked her ex-husband for the money she had loaned him. He demanded to know what she wanted with it and she told him she wanted it to go away and get some medical care. He yelled at her, "When I'm through with you, you won't need anyone's care." Then he grabbed her by the throat and one wrist and tried to choke her. She fell backward but he didn't release his grip on her throat. She managed to get the gun in her free hand and she shot him twice.

The prosecution tried to break her story but she didn't change a word of it. This testimony was in exact opposition to the position the prosecution had taken. But those witnesses could not categorically swear that what Margaret Tuttle said was a lie. Mrs. Tremont Scott, matron of the jail, testified that the next day she had noticed red welts on Mrs. Tuttle's neck.

When all the testimony was in, the jury was instructed and sent out to ponder their verdict. Before they left, each lawyer had his chance to summarize his case to the jury. Attorney Eager from Lincoln was eloquent in his presentation for the defense. He cited the ten hard years his client had spent living with the wild tempered Clifford Tuttle; saying he had abused his young wife constantly. He pleaded for the clemency of the court.. The audience in the courtroom was visibly swayed by his talk. But then Attorney Morrow for the prosecution had the last say, pointing out that the defendant had admitted killing her husband. Life could not be thrown away so cheaply. His cold logic dampened the rhetoric of the defense lawyer.

Scottsbluff County Courthouse, Gering
Courtesy Nebraska State Historical Society

The jury brought back a verdict of third degree murder or manslaughter. This carried a penalty of from one to ten years in the penitentiary. Many thought that if the case had gone to the jury before Attorney Morrow had made his speech that Margaret Tuttle would have gone free. As it was, her penalty was light. She had already been incarcerated in jail since the first of August the year before and that would be taken into consideration in the sentence.

It was a sensational murder trial for Scottsbluff and not many who followed it every day were disappointed in its outcome.

Kamerad Killing—Valley County   1917

World War I was raging in Europe and the United States was approaching its entry into the struggle. On February 8, 1917, a little girl in Ord, Alice Parkos, was murdered. After some time, the murderer, Louis Kamerad, was arrested and put in jail. That should have ended the story except for the trial and sentencing. But it was not to be that easy.

In the first place, feeling was very high over the murder of the little girl. Lynch mobs supposedly didn't take things into their own hands in the civilization of the twentieth century. But those who wanted so much to see the killer swing from a rope were not convinced that the law would mete out the proper punishment for so brutal a crime.

Kamerad's escape from jail on April 4, was equal to an escape from the lynch mob. Whether he had help in escaping jail was of little consequence to the people who were determined to see Kamerad brought to justice. Bloodhounds were brought to the jail to track down the fugitive. It was raining hard but the hounds were not thrown off the track.

The trail led out of town and the sheriff with a big posse followed the hounds. About eleven miles from Ord, the hounds lost the trail and began running in circles, trying to pick up the scent.

Then someone noticed the buggy tracks near the spot where the hounds had become confused. They knew then how Kamerad had eluded the hounds. But they had no idea whether it was an accomplice or just some passerby who had no idea who Kamerad was that had picked up the fugitive and taken him out of harm's way for the moment.

Valley County Courthouse, Ord
Nebraska, Our Towns

The posse headed back into Ord, where the crime had been committed, and there they were given another clue. Someone had broken into a store in town sometime after midnight. Some food and ammunition had been stolen. About the same time, the posse discovered that an automobile had been stolen.

They followed the road that the automobile had taken out of town and some distance from Ord, they found the car, out of gas. The fugitive was gone. They went to the nearest farm house to see if the farmer knew anything about the killer. They found that this farmer's car had been stolen.

The posse followed the muddy tracks down to the main road and saw which way it had gone. They followed as fast as they could go. Only a few miles down the road, they found this car, too. It had been abandoned because of engine trouble.

Again they checked the nearest farm and again they found that the farmer's car had been stolen. The fugitive had headed for Arcadia. But short of town, they found this car abandoned. They were near a farm owned by Pat Brady. In the back seat of the car they found some food and a few cartridges. Apparently Kamerad had abandoned this car in haste and made off on foot.

North Loup in the 1930s
Nebraska, Our Towns

Now they wished for the bloodhounds but they had been left behind after they had lost the trail outside Ord. But a man had seen someone sneaking around Pat Brady's barn and the sheriff took his lantern and headed for the barn. The men who had stuck with the lawman throughout the search were right at his heels. One of the posse was Joe Parkos, the father of the murdered girl. If the posse caught the killer, he intended to be right there to see that he didn't escape again.

With guns in their hands, the men searched the barn carefully. But there was no sign of Kamerad. The sheriff pointed to a cowshed nearby and the entire posse went to it.

Stepping inside, the sheriff held the lantern high to throw light over the interior. Someone spotted a man lying on top of a brace across the rafters. Instantly, all guns were pointed up.

Some posse members recognized Kamerad. The sheriff ordered him to come down and said that he'd protect him.

"I won't come down," Kamerad shouted. "You'd better shoot."

Every man in the posse saw the gun in Kamerad's hand. There was no order to shoot but every gun roared. Kamerad rolled off the brace, dead before he hit the ground.

Joe Parkos was the first man to reach the body. He stared at it and saw that it really was Kamerad and he emptied his gun into the body. It was just as effective as a rope with none of the stigma associated with a lynch mob.

Newkirk Murder—Furnas County   1922

Jack Newkirk of Lenora, Kansas, disappeared from his home on the night of September 6, 1922. His body was found May 5, 1923, south of Beaver City in Furnas County, Nebraska. There was a bullet hole in the skull, and this led to an investigation that brought in many witnesses from both Kansas and Nebraska.

The prime suspect was Woody Turner, who had close connections to the Newkirks. The case required much investigation and preparation, but finally came to the courtroom early in January of 1926.

Although the trial was held at Norton, Kansas, two of the first witnesses were Wade Stevens, county attorney of Furnas County Nebraska, and Sheriff W.E. Bratt, also of Furnas County. Since the body was found in Nebraska, Nebraska authorities had done the initial investigation.

While at first it was considered that the murder had taken place in Nebraska, information came to light that suggested the murder had taken place in Newkirk's home town of Lenora, and the body hauled to Nebraska and dumped where the killer hoped it wouldn't be found for a long time. It had been eight months before it was found. Tom Wells, of Beatrice, was also one of the first witnesses. The Beatrice man testified as to where the body was found, the clothing on the corpse, and the bullet hole in the skull.

Jack Newkirk, Jr. identified the clothing that Sheriff Bratt had found as that of his father. He said the elder Newkirk had been sleeping in the garage for several months before his disappearance.

Detective H.D. Lozier then took the stand and gave some damaging evidence against Turner, Lozier had been put on the trail of Turner and had finally found him in November of 1923. He said that the first thing Turner said when he found him was that he guessed he was after him for the Newkirk murder. Later Turner explained that statement by saying several people had told him they were looking for him and accusing him of Jack Newkirk's murder.

Gideon Hardin, who lived south of Beaver City, told a tale of driving his truck out of Norton, Kansas, the moonlit night of the disappearance of Newkirk, heading for Beaver City. A car followed him for many miles with a mysterious bundle lashed to the running board. The car had no headlights. South of Beaver City, Hardin had engine trouble with his truck and it stopped. He saw that the car that had been following him had stopped a short distance behind so he walked back to see if they would help him.

He saw a man and a woman getting back into the car. They wheeled the car around and sped away toward the Kansas state line. The bundle was no longer on the running board, but Hardin thought nothing of that. He was just disgusted that they had run off without offering to help him.

The defense lawyers asked him which side of the car the bundle was tied to and which side of the truck his steering wheel was on. They got him confused, but he stuck to his story and he said there weren't enough lawyers in the state of Kansas to pry him loose from it.

This testimony was important to the prosecution because their evidence pointed to a love triangle. Jack Newkirk obviously was not getting along well with his wife or he wouldn't have been sleeping in the garage all summer. Woody Turner was present at the Newkirk home quite often and the prosecution was building a case of an amorous connection between Turner and Mrs. Newkirk.

Then came a witness who said he had seen Turner and Mrs. Newkirk meet at an abandoned lumber yard in town several times. Tom Lunney testified that he had found a hat at the old lumber yard right after Newkirk's disappearance. He knew it was Jack Newkirk's because of the way Newkirk always held a crease in his hat with a shingle nail. The theory was that Jack Newkirk had surprised Woody Turner and Mrs. Newkirk in the old lumber yard, and Turner had shot Newkirk in the head. Then the couple had wrapped the body in a bundle, tied it on the running board of Turner's car, and took it north into Nebraska and dumped it.

The defense had an alibi for Mrs. Newkirk, a woman who said Mrs. Newkirk had been at her place all that night. Woody Turner took the stand and explained every bit of evidence against him, making much of it sound very logical.

Evidently the jury was not swayed a great deal by Turner's explanation of the things that the prosecution had brought up. They brought in a verdict of guilty of second degree murder. The verdict was handed down on January 17, 1926. Turner immediately asked for a new trial.

Turner said he had found a new witness who would verify that he had taken Turner to Dellvale to look for a job shucking corn. He presented affidavits to the truth of that testimony. The defense attacked the witness and the testimony. September 6 was too early to begin shucking corn in northern Kansas. Corn had to be dried in the field before it could be cribbed. The lawyers for the defense and the prosecution had a battle of words over the witness and the veracity of his testimony. The judge took everything into consideration and announced he would hand down his decision on a new trial on February 15.

The decision came down and a new trial was denied. But Woody Turner didn't give up easily. He appealed to the state supreme court and brought up still another witness. This one, a man named John Ferney, said that he had been on the road in southern Nebraska the night of September 5, 1922, and a man flagged him down for a ride. He was wild eyed and foaming at the mouth. Ferney refused to let him in the car and drove away. Again affidavits were presented, signed by prominent business men, testifying to the character of John Ferney. But when Ferney said another man had seen the demented man on the road that night, the men who had signed the affidavits realized what was going on and they appeared in court, eleven of them, swearing they wouldn't believe such a story from Ferney even if he was under oath.

Judge Willard Simmons summed up the

evidence and overruled the motion for a new trial.

With all delaying tactics out of the way, Woody Turner was sentenced to twenty years in the penitentiary.

Gordon Murder—Adams County   1923

Pressures often build up and, even though they are comprised of little things, they build to the breaking point. Some insignificant thing may touch them off and they explode into tragedy.

That happened in Hastings on February 21, 1923. The tragedy had been in the making for some time. Dr. Charles Egbert was a skilled surgeon who had moved to Hastings about fifteen years before that fateful day. He had studied at the leading medical centers in Europe. Hastings considered itself fortunate to have him.

Egbert had a daughter who did not follow his wishes when she married. Her husband, Charles (Roy in some reports) Gordon, was an insurance agent but was switching to a job in the oil business when the tragedy occurred.

The Gordons had stayed for a while with the Egberts but had left some time before, due to the antagonism between Gordon and his father-in-law, Dr. Egbert. The Gordons took up temporary residence in the Clarke Hotel.

Dr. Egbert had other troubles, too. His wife had been quite ill for the last three years. Her half sister, Mary Mitchell, had been doing much of the housework as well as taking care of Mrs. Egbert. At this time, Mrs. Egbert was at the Sanitarium. Mary Mitchell was also at the institution, recovering from an operation.

It was all apparently too much for Dr. Egbert. Drugs to keep him going were available to him as a doctor and he apparently was using some.

It was at this juncture that Charles and Mae Gordon stopped by the Egbert house to pick up some of their personal belongings that they had left there when they moved away from the Egbert home. Mrs. Gordon, Egbert's daughter, had a key to the house so she unlocked the door and went inside, calling for her father.

Dr. Egbert appeared from the next room and Mae explained that they had come for some of the things they had left here. He said that was fine for her to come in and get them but that her husband could not come into his house. He wasn't welcome.

Charles Gordon had stopped at the doorway but then he came on in, apparently intent on helping his wife get what she had come for. Dr. Egbert crossed to the door, picking up a pistol from the parlor as he passed. Determination met determination. Gordon was determined to help his wife get their possessions and Dr. Egbert was determined that Gordon should not come into his house again.

Not even Mae Gordon could tell much about the struggle between the two, if there really was a struggle. But when Dr. Egbert saw that he couldn't stop Gordon from coming in even after he had told him he couldn't, he used the pistol. He shot only once but it was a deadly shot through the heart. Charles Gordon was killed almost instantly.

The fury that had snapped the doctor's restraint disappeared like a flash and he rushed out into the yard, his loud cries bringing the neighbors on the run. He was sobbing that he didn't mean to kill him. One of the neighbors coaxed the doctor over to her house while someone called a doctor and the sheriff. The coroner came with the sheriff.

Dr. Smith gave Dr. Egbert a sedative and Sheriff Harm took him to the jail. The circumstances leading up to the shooting were bandied about among his neighbors. They knew that the doctor had been bitterly opposed to his daughter marrying Gordon and that the two men had never gotten along, but none had immagined it could lead to murder. One neighbor, a man named Yocum, reported that Dr. Egbert had been acting strangely for some time. It was suspected that he might have been using some of the prescription drugs that he was supposed to issue sparingly to patients who were in need of them.

Dr. Egbert was disoriented after he got to the jail but by the next morning, he seemed rational and he and his lawyer agreed that he would plead self defense.

But when the arraignment came up a week after the shooting, Dr. Egbert was in such a physical and mental state that they had to carry him into the courtroom on a stretcher. The charge was murder in the first degree. When Judge Turbyfill asked how he would plead, the lawyer replied that they would enter no plea but stand mute. As in such cases, the judge entered a plea of not guilty. Egbert's attorney, L.B. Stiner, asked for a set bail so they could take Dr. Egbert to a hospital. Judge Turbyfill overruled the request and ordered Egbert held in the county jail.

In June the district court convened and Dr. Egbert's trial came up. The trial lasted three days and the courtroom was crowded every day. Dr. Egbert took the stand in his own defense on the last day of the trial. He said he didn't remember the shooting or whether he did it or not. This gave rise to the probability of the doctor having used some of his drugs just before the encounter with his son-in-law.

The case went to the jury the afternoon of Monday, June 25. Their verdict came in about ten o'clock the next morning. The verdict was guilty of murder in the second degree.

A few days later Judge Dilworth sentenced Dr. Egbert to fifteen years in the penitentiary.

Phegley Murder—Adams County 1924

William Phegley and his wife, Laura, lived in Platte County north of the Loup River, near St. Edwards. There was little harmony on their farm and Laura Phegley finally left her husband, got a divorce, and went down near Roseland and got a job as housekeeper for Peter Evans on his farm. The year was 1922.

Lincoln Avenue, Roseland, 1915, boardwalks and dirt street
Nebraska, Our Towns

Phegley brooded over that divorce for a couple of years. Then one day he drove down to Adams County and out to Evans' farm southwest of Roseland just to see his ex-wife.

He found Laura Phegley in the house and Peter Evans was there, too. Phegley had little to say. He simply pulled out a revolver and began shooting at his former wife. He fired three times and all three bullets hit her. She was only a few feet from him when he began shooting. Two of the bullets hit her in the chest; the third hit her right arm.

Evans was nearby, and later, when he reported the incident, he couldn't remember whether Phegley shot at him or not. He did remember dashing outside and getting behind the garage.

As soon as Laura fell, William Phegley hurried back to his car and drove away. There was no chance of his not being identified. He drove directly to Hastings to the police station and turned himself in.

Before he went to town, Evans sent word to the sheriff, and Sheriff Harm, along with Deputy Cole, made a fast trip to Evans' farm beyond Roseland. They had barely arrived there when they got word that Phegley had turned himself in.

Laura Phegley was taken to the Mary Lanning Hospital in Hastings where she wasn't given much chance to survive.

In the meantime, William Phegley was being questioned. He gave very little reason for shooting his ex-wife. He did repeat: "He broke up my home." They assumed he was referring to Peter Evans. But why he shot his wife instead of Evans was something he didn't explain.

The shooting occurred on Saturday, April 5, 1924. By Monday, Laura Phegley was still alive, but her condition was considered extremely serious. On Tuesday, she was better and some hope was held out for her recovery. But during the night, her condition took a turn for the worse and she died at 3:15 Wednesday morning.

County attorney Crow changed his charge against William Phegley from attempted murder to first degree murder.

Phegley was arraigned before Judge Turbyfill and pled not guilty. However, he did waive a hearing. The judge bound him over to the next district court. Since the charge was first degree murder, no bail was allowed. He was taken back to jail to await the spring session of the district court.

At that session of the court, Phegley was tried and convicted by a jury of second degree murder. Many had trouble understanding how the jury could bring a verdict of second degree murder when it had every appearance of premeditated murder.

Main Street of Ayr, in 1901
Nebraska, Our Towns

Convicted only of second degree murder, Phegley drew a sentence of twelve years in the penitentiary.

A couple of years later, from his prison cell, Phegley filed a suit against Peter Evans for twenty-five thousand dollars for alienating the affections of Laura Phegley, and thus contributing to such terrible grief to Phegley that it led to his killing his ex-wife.

Evans was still living in the same community but with his address at Ayr now instead of Roseland. He denied having anything to do with the domestic troubles of the Phegleys. He said that when he hired Mrs. Phegley as his housekeeper, he did not know her at all.

Judge Dilworth presided at this trial and rendered a verdict in favor of Evans. William Phegley was faced now with finishing out his term in prison.

Moore Murder—Adams County 1924

Carl Moore, an automobile salesman in Hastings, was going about his regular business when he disappeared on October 16, 1924. That day he had a potential customer down in Roseland, twelve to fifteen miles southwest of Hastings.

He drove the new car out of Hastings that he hoped to sell to a man named Roberts, at Roseland. A couple of young men went with him. No one knew why he took those men with him since they would hardly be of any help to him in selling the car.

When Moore failed to return to Hastings that night, search parties began going out, looking for him or the new car he had taken. Nothing was found. There were few who would believe that Moore had absconded with the new car. He was not that kind of man.

On Saturday, November 1, J.W. Markin, superintendent of the Roseland school, went out hunting. He stumbled onto the body of Moore in a plum thicket in a rather deserted section of country, two or three miles northeast of Roseland.

Markin forgot about his hunting, hurried back to town, and notified Adams County authorities. Then he accompanied Deputy Sheriff Guy Cole, County Attorney Crow, and Dr. Smith to the site.

The murder shocked those who knew Moore, yet it was not such a great surprise—

General merchandise store before
1925, Roseland
Nebraska, Our Towns

since they'd had two weeks to ponder what could have happened to him—but it was a mystery as to who had murdered Moore. He had been killed by a blow from a heavy instrument to the left side of his head. A machinist's hammer was found close to the body.

That hammer proved to be an important clue. They discovered that the hammer was missing from Harvey Breckner's tool chest. Two young men had been staying with the Breckners for a few days. They were gone now. Those two were suspected of murdering Moore, but their only possible motive anyone could see was to steal the new car that Moore had been taking to Roseland.

The two men were not well known around town. Those who knew the names they used suspected they were fakes. Authorities decided they must know something about the country because they had picked one of the most isolated spots in the county to hide the body, the plum thicket on Frank Folksdorf's farm.

Chief of Police Branagan, of Hastings, took it on himself to find these murderers, if possible. Sure that the two men had killed Moore to get the new car, he tried to find the auto. He finally located it where it had been abandoned at Wilbur, southwest of Lincoln, in Saline County. Some people there said they saw two people get out of that car and go in different directions. That information wasn't exactly helpful to Branagan. Further investigation indicated that the two had gotten together again and caught a train to Lincoln.

In Lincoln, Branagan learned that two men, one answering the description of one of the men Branagan wanted, had visited his sister. Now Branagan had the real name of one of the men; Donald Ringer.

Branagan learned that Ringer had another sister in Gulfport, Mississippi. So he headed for Mississippi. In the little town of Lyman, just north of Gulfport, Branagan caught up with Ringer. He sent a telegram back to Nebraska that he had the suspect in custody. He didn't say how he intended to bring him back to Nebraska, but they assumed that he would.

Donald Ringer was only nineteen years

Sacred Heart Catholic Church, Roseland, built in 1921
Nebraska, Our Towns

old. He told Branagan that the man who had been with him, George Bender, was about twenty-two. Bender wasn't with Ringer when Branagan caught him, and Ringer thought he had left the county for far-away places.

Branagan got a confession out of Ringer. He admitted that he had killed Carl Moore. There was no legal objection to bringing him back to Nebraska. Feelings were still high around Adams County when Branagan returned with the suspect.

Donald Ringer was arraigned before Adams County Judge Turbyfill and was bound over to District court. No bail was allowed. District court was scheduled to convene sometime in April.

It seems likely that George Bender had been with Ringer in Belleville, Illinois, because Bender's parents lived there. It apparently had been on one of Ringer's visits to see his sister in Belleville that Ringer and Bender got acquainted and began traveling together. But now Bender had disappeared like fog in hot sunshine.

In Ringer's confession, he divulged some of

the details surrounding the murder. The reason for getting rid of Carl Moore had been to get the car he was trying to sell. It was Bender who wanted the car to make a trip to Texas. But, according to Ringer, Bender wasn't present at the time that Ringer used the hammer to kill Moore. Ringer said he had hit Moore first with his fist and stunned him then gave him a light tap with the hammer. He just wanted to put him out long enough to get away with the car. When he saw that Moore was dead, Ringer took him to the plum thicket and put him there, thinking it would be some time before anyone found him. In that, he was right.

According to Ringer, Bender didn't even come with him when he accompanied Moore to Roseland. Yet witnesses at the garage in Hastings said both men went with Moore when he left to demonstrate the car in Roseland. Ringer said that Bender was to meet him at the scene of the tragedy but didn't show up. So he drove back to Hastings, didn't find Bender, then left Hastings on the D-L-D (Detroit-Lincoln-Denver) Highway, going east. When he hit a place where road work was being done and was shunted off on a detour, he went down to Wilbur. Here he took the train to Lincoln. Here again witnesses said there were two men who got out of the car in Wilbur. The abandoned car was Branagan's first step in running down Donald Ringer.

One police officer who helped with the questioning said he thought that Ringer was afraid of Bender and was trying to shield him from any guilt in the murder. Ringer's past record was not going to help him in his defense. He had been sent to the reform School in 1917.

By the time the questioning ended, Ringer was getting very nervous. One officer thought that Ringer was just beginning to realize the seriousness of the trouble he was in.

At the trial in district court, Ringer entered

a plea of not guilty in spite of his earlier confession. His attorney, J.E. Willits of Hastings, put up a great defense of Ringer but the evidence was too strong. His earlier confession and description of the way things happened were too much, and he was convicted of first degree murder. The verdict brought about a sentence of death in the electric chair.

Willits appealed the case to the state supreme court, which gave the evidence a careful scrutiny. They refused to change the verdict and the execution date was set for July 9, 1926.

Blanche Davis Murder— Furnas County 1925

Blanche Davis died on August 30, 1925, at Beaver City, Nebraska. But that was just the beginning, not the end, of the story. Blanche and Bert Davis had been married in 1898 and had four children. No one suspected that Mrs. Davis was in bad health.

There were unusual circumstances surrounding her death and, while most people accepted the facts as they appeared to be, others questioned them. Sheriff Bratt of Furnas County had an autopsy made on Mrs. Davis. The surprising thing that came of that was the strychnine that was found in her stomach.

The first reaction was that she had committed suicide. But no one could recall any reason why she might have done that. She had not been depressed or seriously ill. The only other alternative was murder.

That seemed entirely out of order. She had no known enemies. Bert Davis, her husband, had been a well-to-do stockraiser near Beaver City and later operated a grocery store in town. He certainly was not one to be suspected of murdering his wife of more than a quarter of a century.

But suspicion lingered. It revived when

Lashley Mill at Beaver City
Nebraska, Our Towns

Bert Davis married Mrs. Kate Ressler in December at Manhattan, Kansas. Mrs. Ressler was a widow who lived right across the street from the Davises in Beaver City.

Sheriff W.E. Bratt began investigating in earnest then. From several sources, he began to hear how Bert Davis had been seen with Mrs. Ressler and had favored her with gifts. His investigation turned up things that made him feel that there was far more to Blanche Davis's death than met the eye.

Bert Davis and his new wife had moved to Lincoln but they were aware of the investigation. Finally, when Sheriff Bratt thought he had enough evidence to warrant arrest, he went to Lincoln to arrest Bert Davis. On the same day, Davis came to

Beaver City to turn himself in and clear up the whole matter. Deputy Sheriff Bonham made the arrest.

Private detectives had been at work and so had the sheriff and his deputy. They brought Bert Davis before County Judge F.E. Vancleve and charged him with first degree murder. He was bound over to district court and held without bail in the county jail. Davis's plea was not guilty, and he said that he and his former wife's relatives had been trying to find the evidence that would verify his innocence.

Furnas County's second courthouse
Nebraska, Our Towns

On February 11, 1926, Mrs. Ressler-Davis was arrested. The preliminary hearing for Kate Ressler-Davis was held the next day, Friday, February 12. By now the populace was stirred up and the courtroom was packed so full of people that the session had to be moved to the larger district court room.

Many witnesses were called to testify at the hearing. Bert Davis's son, Glen, said his

father bought a $275 ring and gave it to the defendant, Mrs. Ressler-Davis, and he identified some letters found in her home as the hand writing of his father.

Dr. J.T. Meyers of Omaha Medical College testified that he had found strychnine in the stomach of the dead woman. Mrs. Beulah Kingman said she had visited Kate Ressler one day and had opened a closet door and found Bert Davis hiding there. County Extension Agent W.R. Wicks testified that he had sold strychnine poison to Davis to kill gophers on Davis's farm, and identified a box of the poison as one like those from his office.

Others testified to seeing Bert Davis go to Mrs. Ressler's home and remain for an hour or two. Two ladies, named Wilson, testified that they had roomed with Mrs. Ressler from the fall of 1924 till the spring of 1925 and had read a letter from Mrs. Ressler addressed to Bert Davis, advising him to "treat her like a loving neighbor until sometime when they might become something sweeter."

There were several more who testified, all things pointing to the involvement of Mrs. Ressler in the death of Mrs. Davis—if that proved to be murder.

At the end of the hearing, the defense attorneys asked that the case against Mrs. Ressler-Davis be dismissed. Since there had not yet been proved any charge against Bert Davis, there could hardly be a charge of being an accessory lodged against their client.

John Stevens, attorney for the prosecution, objected to the motion and pointed to the evidence that had been presented. Judge Vancleve overruled the motion by the defense and ordered the defendant held without bail until district court convened. District Court was scheduled to convene March 22, 1926.

The trial came up at the district court session on March 25. Judge Eldridge granted a change of venue for Bert Davis to McCook on April 26, and for Kate Davis to Elwood on May 13.

Winter day in McCook
*Courtesy County Historical
Society, McCook*

Apparently when Bert Davis returned to Beaver City to give himself up, he felt that it would be a simple matter to prove his innocence; but when he got into district court, he learned that there was far more evidence stacked up against him than he had anticipated. As the headline in the May 6 paper declared: "Davis fighting for his life."

The jury at McCook finally got the order to make a decision on Bert Davis's guilt on the afternoon of May 6. It had been a long trial, and the jury had been instructed to decide whether Bert Davis was guilty of first degree murder or not. It was either guilty or acquittal. The jury stayed out for fifty hours, debating and taking ballots. There was some fluctuation in the balloting, but there were some who were absolutely convinced that he was guilty and there were at least two who could not be swayed from an acquittal verdict. The trial had begun on April 26 and had not gone to jury until May 6. With a "hung jury" the trial came to an end.

It left many doubts, but a second trial ended in another "hung jury," so the doubts remained.

Maryott—Garden County 1926

If ever there were two people under one skin, it was so in Miles J. Maryott. A nice looking, upstanding man when he was sober; a raving maniac capable of murder when he was drinking. Some people pointed to Maryott as the perfect example of what drinking can do to a man. Children were warned, using Maryott as a model, to stay away from the bottle.

Miles Maryott was born in 1871 in Tekamah, Nebraska, close to the Missouri River. By the time he was in school, his family lived in Cozad, along the Platte River east of North Platte. He left school after the tenth grade and turned to baseball, playing professional ball in the minor leagues in the 1890s, in Minnesota, Illinois, Colorado, and Kansas.

He became an expert shot and won some national shooting contests. That brought him some notice. In 1909, he took a Kinkaid homestead north of Oshkosh. The Kinkaid differed from a regular homestead in that it

Typical sod house, the kind most homesteaders in Nebraska built

Courtesy Jane Graff

included a full section of land, 640 acres, while a regular homestead was just 160 acres. By the early 1900s, the good farm land was gone. Only the poor land was left. Some men, if given a full section of that poor land, were willing to try to make a living on it. Maryott was one of those.

Miles Maryott was also a painter. He had been drawing since he was a boy. Wildlife was his favorite subject and he became quite good at painting scenes of wildlife in Nebraska's wide open spaces.

But in acquiring so many skills, he also acquired a habit that led to his ruin. He developed a taste for alcohol and yielded to its invitation, in spite of the fact that just one drink turned him into a wild man. Anger drove him and he was seized by an urge to destroy.

Many times he was arrested for disturbing the peace, which was a mild way of describing his tantrums when he was drunk. Often, in jail after he sobered up, he would paint a picture and use it for his bail. Jailers, sheriffs, and judges valued his paintings, for they were extraordinary.

But then came the fateful day in Oshkosh: Wednesday, November 24, 1926, the day before Thanksgiving. Maryott had had some drinks and, as always, he became a different man from the mild-mannered painter that his friends knew.

He was driving down the street, raving mad, just after school was out for the day

Oshkosh Land & Cattle Company General Store & Post Office, originally built in 1889

Nebraska, Our Towns

and saw E.W. McCall, superintendent of the high school. Stopping his car, he shouted at McCall, threatening to kill him if he didn't go straight home and walk a straight line doing it. He also threatened to kill the county attorney.

McCall hurried toward home but as soon as Maryott had driven on, he turned to call the town marshal, George Albee, and demanded that he arrest Maryott before he carried out some of his threats.

Albee had been called on before to arrest Maryott. It wasn't a pleasant task because there was no telling what Maryott would do when he was drunk. But he set out to find Maryott, knowing that wouldn't be hard to do. Maryott was not one to hide when he was drunk. He let the world know where he was and informed everyone within hearing distance that he was king of the walk.

Albee found Maryott on the main street,

still swaggering and threatening anyone he saw. Albee called on Maryott to stop, saying he was under arrest. Maryott used his revolver, firing at the marshal. The bullet missed but it warned Albee that this time Maryott was wilder than usual. That shot hadn't been a warning shot. Maryott had just missed because he was so drunk.

Albee fired at Maryott, aiming low so as not to kill him. He hit him in the leg. But that didn't sober up Maryott. He fired again, coming frighteningly close to the marshal. Albee fired back. They exchanged a couple of shots and Albee hit Maryott in the side with one bullet. Albee was no longer trying to keep from killing Maryott. Maryott was definitely trying to kill Albee.

Maryott went down from the bullet in his side. Albee approached cautiously, thinking that his last shot had probably killed Maryott. Reaching the fallen man, he leaned over to see if the man was dead. Maryott suddenly whipped up his revolver and shot the marshal twice in the chest. Albee was killed instantly. He left a wife and several children.

Some said that the reason Maryott was so wild this time was that he had had a fight with Bud Aufdengarten a few days before over killing some wild ducks out of season. In the fight, Maryott had been knocked down and he hadn't forgotten it. On this day, one report said, Maryott had fired once into the apartment of Bud Aufdengarten. This was just before Marshal Albee confronted him.

Maryott was taken to the doctor's office to have his wounds dressed. They were serious but not life threatening. There were murmurings among the men of Oshkosh. Marshal Albee had been a respected man in town. But if there was talk of lynching, cooler heads put a stop to it. After all, the day of rope justice had passed thirty years ago.

Maryott was tried and sentenced to life imprisonment. That was one prison sentence that did profit many future generations. Miles Maryott had mounted nearly fifteen hundred specimens of wild birds and animals in his day as a taxidermist. Now he could only paint those denizens of the wild. His paintings while he was in prison lost none of their natural poise because he was no longer in touch with them. Maryott's paintings hold prominent positions today in displays in many places in Nebraska. Many of his mounted birds and animals are on display in the museum in Oshkosh.

Maryott developed cirrhosis of the liver and, early in 1939, he was granted a pardon so he could go home to die. He died on December 20, 1939, and is buried in Fairview Cemetery near Cozad.

BIBLIOGRAPHY

BOOKS

Bang, Roy E. *Heroes Without Medals—A Pioneer History of Kearney County.* Minden, Nebraska: Warp Publishing Co., 1952.
Wilson, D. Ray. *Nebraska Historical Tour Guide.* Carpenterville, Illinois: Crossroads Communications, 1988.

MAGAZINES

Yost, Nellie. "Land Fraud and Murder in the Sandhills." *American West,* August, 1988.

NEWSPAPERS

Adams County Democrat. February 23, 1923; March 2, 1923; June 28, 1923; July 5, 1923.
Beaver City Times-Tribune. February 28, 1926; March 6, 1926; March 25, 1926; May 13, 1926.
County Pioneer-Lexington. December 3, 1926.
Farmer's Gazette. June, 1927.
Hastings Democrat. April 10, 1924; April 17, 1924; November 6, 1924; December 11, 1924; January 8, 1925; February 12, 1925; April 16, 1925; May 20, 1926; May 27, 1926.
Lincoln State Journal. February 14, 1909.
Nebraska State Journal. March 27, 1912; October 13, 1913.
Omaha World-Herald. November 27, 1926.
The Postal Card. Eustis, Nebraska. February 28, 1903.
The Republican. Stockville, Nebraska. October 8, 1903.
Scottsbluff Daily Star-Herald. February 12, 1926.
Scottsbluff Star-Herald. August 3, 1916; August 17, 1916; March 1, 1917; April 5, 1917.
The Times-Tribune. Beaver City, Nebraska. January 21, 1926; February 11, 1926; February 18, 1926.

Index

FORTS AND STATIONS

PEOPLE

TOWNS